S---ts
and
Tracks
of the
Pacific Coast
including British Columbia

A Field Guide to the Signs of 70 Wildlife Species

James C. Halfpenny, Ph.D.

Illustrated by Todd Telander

FALCONGUIDES ®

GUILFORD, CONNECTICUT
HELENA, MONTANA

AN IMPRINT OF THE GLOBE PEQUOT PRESS

FALCONGUIDES®

Copyright © 1999 Morris Book Publishing, LLC
Previously published by Falcon Publishing, Inc.

All black-and-white photos by James C. Halfpenny unless otherwise noted.

Library of Congress Cataloging-in-Publication Data

Halfpenny, James C.
    Scats and tracks of the Pacific Coast states : a field guide to
  the signs of 70 wildlife species / James C. Halfpenny ; illustrated
  by Todd Telander.
      p. cm.
    Includes bibliographical references (p.).
    ISBN 978-1-56044-869-3 (pbk.)
    1. Animal tracks—Pacific Coast (U.S.) 2. Vertebrates—Pacific
  Coast (U.S.) I. Title.
  QL768.H355 1999
  596'0979—dc21   99-25395
                                                                  CIP

Printed in Canada
First edition/Fifth Printing

To Diann, my alpha partner,
ursophile, and tracking friend, for
all her loving support and help.

Acknowledgments

First and foremost, I wish to thank all my students for their years of questions and help, but most of all for the time we've shared tracking and studying in the field. I also wish to thank Dixie Finley, Sue Lane, and Tom Lindsay, as well as Susan Morse (Keeping Track, Jericho, Vermont) for her help with lynx and their footprints.

Contents

Introduction

In the late 1970s, the era of "watchable wildlife" arrived in the United States. Baby boomers wanted to turn to and experience the outdoors. Television brought wildlife closer than ever. Bird watching thrived. Now more than ever, millions of people want to watch wild animals. Wildlife are not always easy to find and observe, though. Finding their tracks and signs is an exciting alternative to actually seeing the animals. "Trackable wildlife" adds a dimension to the outdoor experience. Todd and I wish to share that dimension, the joy of reading stories written in the soil and snow.

Upwards of ten books on tracking have been written in the United States during each decade of the 20th century. Most are general, covering the United States or all of North America. In *Scats and Tracks of the Pacific Coast*, we focus on one biogeographic region, with details about the region's most common or characteristic species of mammals, birds, reptiles, and amphibians. (We have included a few rare species because of their particular interest or significance in a region. For example, what a coup it would be to document a grizzly bear in Washington.) We've intentionally limited the number of species covered in order to keep the information manageable. This guide is small, allowing you to carry it in a pack or pocket and use it frequently.

As your knowledge and interest in tracking grows, you may want to find additional information and help. Key references are listed in the Selected Readings. For a more detailed investigation of tracking, I recommend my book *A Field Guide to Mammal Tracking in North America* (1986, Johnson Publishing, Boulder, CO), and titles by Olaus Murie, L. R. Forrest, and Paul Rezendes.

Two organizations will, in computer parlance, provide interactive access to expand your tracking background. A

Naturalist's World (ANW) is an ecologically oriented company dedicated to providing educational programs and materials reflecting the natural history of North America. Diann Thompson and I run the daily business, teach classes, and lead programs. Our on-site classes provide hands-on experience and in-depth information about animals, their tracks, and the ecology of their environments. In addition to tracking classes, our field programs cover bears, wolves, winter ecology, the northern lights, and alpine ecology. ANW also provides books, videos, slides shows, and computer programs for self-study and as teaching and field aids. You can check out ANW on the internet at www.tracknature.com.

The Tracker's Research Association (TRAck) is the research and tracking communication branch of ANW. TRAck's purpose is to provide

1) communication among trackers,

2) continued opportunities for individuals to hone their tracking skills and knowledge,

3) research into the science of tracking.

TRAck is a scientific organization conceived to facilitate quality knowledge in the field of tracking. The scope of TRAck spans the broadest concept of the science of tracking, including not only tracking skills, but the social, philosophical, and management aspects of tracking. TRAck communicates through its newsletter.

Class schedules, product information, and information about ANW and TRAck can be obtained from P.O. Box 989, Gardiner, Montana 59030, phone (406) 848-9458, or on the worldwide web at www.tracknature.com.

Keep on tracking!

—James C. Halfpenny

About tracking

Tracking is for everyone, beginner and expert, young and old. The fun of nature's challenge is solving the mystery written in the trail. Prepare yourself by learning the backgrounds and basics of tracking before exercising your skills in the field.

Field notes and preserving tracks

To the natural history detective, the track and trail are things of great beauty and significance. They tell part of the story of an animal's life. Tracks and trails deserve to be preserved, both to increase your knowledge and as a record you can share with others. Preservation is commonly made in the form of written notes, casts, or photographs.

Perhaps the most important item in the naturalist's tool kit is the field notebook. Field notes can jog the memory and facilitate better retention of knowledge. The notes can be analyzed later and can be preserved as records of chance encounters. Writing good field notes is an art form and a science in itself. Field notes are a source of pride when shown to others and may gain recognition for recording rare and unusual events. And need I mention how quickly memories, especially for details, fade when not preserved?

While great and complex systems have been designed for complete and accurate records, there are really but three requirements for the tracker: ruler, paper, and pen. With these, every trail becomes a record for later analysis and sharing. I cannot emphasize enough the importance of enhancing your tracking experience by keeping notes to which you can later refer!

A simple 3-inch by 5-inch notebook and a 6-inch ruler are adequate to get started. Use a pencil or a pen that won't run if your notes get wet. To facilitate taking notes, A

Naturalist's World produces a waterproof notebook that contains information about footprint groups, gaits, and how to track; data sheets for recording information; and English and metric rulers imprinted on the back cover. See the Introduction for contact information for A Naturalist's World.

Tracks may also be preserved by photographing and making casts. Good photographs can be made by any modern camera that can take a good close-up. When taking pictures, try to fill the viewfinder with the footprint. Get as close as possible. Always include a ruler or some other object in the photo to provide a sense of scale. Avoid using hats, gloves, hands, or objects without a straight edge; round edges do not lend themselves to making accurate measurements from a photo. To avoid distortion, take the photograph from directly above the track, shooting straight down. Also, step back and take photographs of the trail to show the footprints that were photographed close-up. Fast films (ASA of 200 or higher) are generally best, because tracks are often found in dark places, especially ground surfaces.

Plaster casts are the old standby for preserving tracks. I suggest a casting kit that includes a 1-gallon (4-liter) plastic jar with a screw lid for carrying dry plaster, a narrow spatula, a plastic mixing cup such as those sold for medium-sized drinks, paper for wrapping and transporting the finished cast, and a plastic sack for cleanup. A bottle of water may be needed if water is not available on-site. Two pounds of plaster will make at least four coyote-sized track casts.

Purchase plaster from a lumberyard or hardware store, as prices will be more reasonable than at a drugstore or hobby shop. Almost any plaster will work, including plaster of paris, hydrocal, ultracal, or hydrostone. Avoid getting plaster for wallboard or patching compound, however. These plasters are formulated to be slightly flexible on walls and do not get hard enough for casts.

Two factors are critical to preventing casts from breaking: thickness and density. In the field, thickness is assured by building a wall around the track to contain the plaster. Natural objects such as twigs, stones, and dirt may be used to make a retaining wall 0.25–0.5 in (0.6–1.3 cm) above the track. Alternatively, walls in the form of plastic strips cut from milk cartons or other plastic containers may be brought to the field. Proper density is assured by mixing two parts of plaster to one part of water by volume (read instructions on plaster container) to create a mixture similar in consistency to thick pancake batter or a milkshake.

Place your spatula close to the track and pour onto the spatula to break the fall of the plaster into the footprint. Working quickly, so the plaster does not set and become too thick, gently pour the plaster first into the fine detailed areas of the footprint and then the rest of the print. Finally, pour the plaster to an appropriate depth (inside the retaining wall) to keep the cast from breaking. Vibrating the spatula up and down across the top of the plaster will cause it to settle evenly and create a smooth back for the cast.

Allow the plaster to dry for 30 minutes, or as long as is recommended on the plaster package. Gently pick the plaster up by digging your fingers under opposite sides of the cast, and turn the cast over onto one hand. Now wash off the dirt by rubbing the cast with your fingertips under the flowing water of a stream or a hose. Do not wash the cast in a sink as it may clog the drain. Let the cast continue to cure for several days in a warm, dry environment. If you need to transport it, wrap the cast in paper. Never wrap it in plastic as trapped moisture may cause it to crumble.

While special techniques are needed for dust and snow, this procedure will allow casting in many situations. Remember, carry a plastic garbage bag and *always* clean up your mess. No sign of your plaster should remain to reduce the experience of others who happen by later.

Scats and bird pellets

Scats and bird pellets (also called cough pellets or castings) are often helpful for identifying an animal or completing the story written in the trail. Scats and pellets help identify not only what the animal was eating, but who the animal was. However, it should be noted that scats and pellets won't help you identify an animal with as much certainty as tracks will. Many animals make similar scats and pellets that are difficult to tell apart.

The scats of many carnivores are very similar, especially when the diet is mostly meat. Size alone does not provide a definitive answer because of the wide range of diameters produced within a species and even by a single member of a species. For example, fox produce scats ranging in size from 0.3–0.8 in (0.8–2 cm), coyotes produce scats from 0.5–1.3 in (1.3–3.3 cm), and wolves produce scats from 0.5–1.5 in (1.3–3.8 cm), and we all know how our own scat varies in size and shape. When judging size, consider both the total quantity of scat and the size of individual pieces. Moist food produces slimmer scats, while fibrous diets produce wider scats.

Given these cautions, scat shapes can be used to identify general groups of animals (see page xii). Spherical shapes flattened top to bottom are deposited by members of the rabbit order. Elongate spheres are deposited by rodents and shrews, and at larger sizes by deer and their relatives. Long, thick cords are deposited by dogs, bears, and raccoons. Dog scats typically have tapered ends, while those from bears and raccoons are blunt. Cats also produce thick cords with blunt ends, but they tend to be constricted or even broken into short segments. Cords that loop back on themselves are produced by members of the weasel family. Birds, in general, produce long, thin cords or shapeless, semiliquid excretions. Reptiles and amphibians may produce small elongate spheres or long, thin cords. White, nitrogenous urine deposits, found only on the scats of birds, reptiles, and amphibians, separate them from mammal scats.

Scats may be confused with cough pellets. Many bird groups, including owls, raptors, crows, ravens, jays, magpies, gulls, herons, storks, flycatchers, and kingfishers, produce cough pellets in addition to scats. Birds pass digestive juices through what they have eaten to remove the nutrients. Hair, bones, beaks, claws, and other non-digestible parts accumulate in the gizzard (anterior portion of stomach), are compressed, and are coughed up as pellets. Food remnants in the pellet are easy to identify and tell much about the bird's feeding habits and even the habitats it frequents.

cough pellet

Pellets are grayish in color and are spherical or long and tapered at both ends. When fresh, they are covered by mucus and appear dark black. Pellets are found mainly at roosting sites and nests, and occasionally at feeding areas. They are deposited singly, but many may accumulate beneath a tree where a bird is roosting, nesting, or perching. Nitrogenous scat deposits on the ground or twigs may help verify an object as a pellet.

The diameter of the throat determines the maximum diameter of the pellet. In general, large birds produce larger pellets. Shape and diameter allow one to distinguish to some degree between species.

Birds generally produce two pellets per day and regurgitate just before taking flight. The time of day when feeding occurred may affect the sample of food items. For example, owls tend to feed on mammals that come out only at night, while hawks feed on animals that are out during the daylight hours.

Shapes of scats

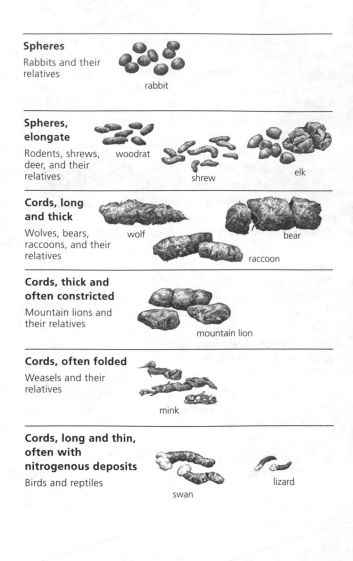

Spheres

Rabbits and their relatives

rabbit

Spheres, elongate

Rodents, shrews, deer, and their relatives

woodrat

shrew

elk

Cords, long and thick

Wolves, bears, raccoons, and their relatives

wolf

bear

raccoon

Cords, thick and often constricted

Mountain lions and their relatives

mountain lion

Cords, often folded

Weasels and their relatives

mink

Cords, long and thin, often with nitrogenous deposits

Birds and reptiles

swan

lizard

Anatomy and footprint nomenclature

The feet of mammals, birds, reptiles, and amphibians are anatomically complex, and that complexity shows in their footprints. Knowing something of the anatomy of their feet will aid in footprint identification and interpreting trails.

The toes of all animals are numbered from the inside of the foot out (the inside of the foot being the side closest to the animal). Therefore, in humans and other mammals, the thumb or big toe (if present) is number 1 and the little finger or little toe is number 5. In birds, toe 1 (if present) points backward.

Over evolutionary time, toes of animals have become reduced in size or have disappeared altogether. In cats and dogs, toe 1 is absent or reduced to a small toe called a *dewclaw*. In deer, elk, sheep, and similar mammals, toe 1 is absent and toes 2 and 5 are reduced and form dewclaws. Toes 3 and 4, the *clouts*, form the cloven *hoof*. In pronghorn antelope, toes 1, 2, and 5 are absent. In birds, toe 5 is absent and toe 1 is often reduced, and occasionally is absent. In the reptiles and amphibians covered here, toe 1 has been lost from the front foot.

Track measurements

To more accurately determine the size of an animal's foot from its tracks, mountain lion researchers Fjelline and Mansfield (1989) developed what we call the "minimum outline" method of measuring tracks.

Place your hand on a hard surface, a table for instance. Note the contact area of your hand with that surface. If your hand went no deeper into that surface, your handprint would have only one size—the *minimum outline*. If your hand were to sink deeper into the surface—as it would if the surface were, say, mud—it would create a series of variable outlines, each larger than the one before, as the mud flowed around the curved surface of your hand. All footprints have a minimum outline, but only prints that sink into a surface have variable outlines.

Note that while the variable outline of a footprint may only be several millimeters wider than the minimum outline, those few millimeters have a large visual effect. The human eye sees area, and area increases with the square of a linear measurement. In short, a few millimeters of width adds a lot of area to a footprint.

The minimum outline size does not change for different surfaces, and therefore provides a standard for comparison between surfaces. And though one animal may leave many sizes of footprints depending on surface, slope, and speed, there is only one minimum outline for every footprint an animal might leave. The minimum outline measurement is the only constant and consistent size in tracking.

To measure the minimum outline, study the bottom of a print. The *break point* where the rounded pad turns upward is the edge of the minimum outline. Use this edge to measure tracks.

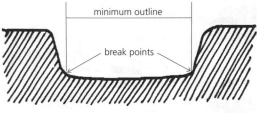

cross section of footprint in ground

Assigning the break point is a subjective judgment and no two people will always mark it at exactly the same point. However, testing has shown that an individual tracker using the minimum outline method can reduce personal variation in measurement, and that groups of trackers using this method will also become more consistent in their measurement of tracks. Quality measurements are the tracker's goal, and using minimum outline methods greatly reduces over-exaggeration and variance in measurement.

All measurements in this guide are minimum outline measurements.

The measurements in *Scats and Tracks of the Pacific Coast* are mostly averages gathered from years of tracking. Averages include only animals judged to be adult. However, it is important to remember that there is great variation in size among animals. Every animal was small once in its life, and some never get big. Males are often substantially larger than females. Regional variations in mammal sizes also occur. For example, coyotes are smaller in the southwestern United States and larger in the northeastern part of the country. Their tracks vary accordingly. Therefore, a track in the field may be considerably larger or smaller than the measurements provided. Use track measurements only as a rough guideline, not as an absolute rule.

Gaits and trails

Coordinated muscle movements result in the various gaits used by animals. In the simplest form, when moving on two legs—bipedal movement—an organism can *walk, run,* and *hop.* When moving on four legs—quadrupedal movement—an organism can walk, *trot, lope, gallop, bound,* and *pronk* (also called *stot*). Though other gaits exist, we will confine our discussion to these basics. Each gait leaves a characteristic pattern that may be modified by changes in speed and body angle. The combination of footprints is called the *trail.* The bipedal walk and run and the quadrupedal walk and trot result in gaits that are *symmetrical:* The right side of the trail is a mirror image of the left side. The trail patterns for these gaits are the same, alternating right-left pattern, and they differ only by the stride being longer in the run and trot than it is in the walk. In the run and trot, the *straddle,* the distance from the right edge of the rightmost *pad* (see page xix) to the left edge of the leftmost pad, also tends to be narrower than it is in the walk.

Quadrupedal movement also results in gaits that are *asymmetrical* (the right half of the trail is *not* a mirror image of the left), including lope, gallop, bound, hop, and pronk. These gaits result in patterns that include all four footprints (two fronts, two hinds, two rights, and two lefts) in a group separated from the next group by a space where no footprints appear.

walk   trot

In *gallops,* the feet, front and rear, that move first (or *lead*) will determine whether the gallop will form a Z-shaped or C-shaped pattern. When the front and hind feet on the same side lead, the pattern takes on a Z shape. A right front lead with a left hind lead or vice versa results in a C-shaped pattern. Thus, there are four possible gallop patterns.

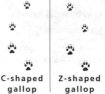

C-shaped   Z-shaped
gallop   gallop

Bounds (also known as hops and jumps) are characterized by the synchronization of the hind feet; both strike the ground at the same time, side by side. The front feet strike the ground at a different time than the hind feet. In a full bound, the front feet are synchronized and strike the ground side by side at the same time. In a half bound, only the hind feet are synchronized and the front feet hit the ground staggered. Animals that mostly use full bounds, also called "hops," live in trees (tree squirrels

full   half
bound   bound

and songbirds), whereas those that mostly use half bounds live on the ground (ground squirrels and rabbits).

In a *pronk* (also called a *stot*), all four feet strike the ground at the same time, with the front feet side by side and forward of the hind feet, which are also

side by side. This gait is often used by deer to gain height and increase time in the air to look around.

To allow for peripheral vision, non-primate mammals have eyes placed toward the side of their heads, not flat on their face like humans. By turning sideways, a prey species can see what is pursuing it and where it needs to go to escape. The predator, by turning sideways, can see what it is chasing and where the rest of the predator pack is.

slow side trot

side gallop

Consequently, quadrupedal mammals have evolved to use all gaits while their body is turned to the side. These *side gaits* result when the animal's heavy head deviates from the line of travel and the body turns sideways. First, the front feet respond by moving toward the side of the trail where the head is. Then, as the head turns more, the hind feet move to the side away from the head. The greater the head movement, the greater the angle of the side gait. Common examples are the side trot and side gallop often used by canids. This is often called a "dog trot" or "dog gallop."

An animal's size is also reflected in its gait patterns. When a mammal is walking with its normal gait, for example, the stride is 1.1 to 1.25 times larger than the distance from the hip to the shoulder joint. Using this crude relationship, body size can be judged from a walking stride. An 18–20 in (45–50 cm) stride indicates a hip-to-shoulder length of 22 in (55 cm). Add to the hip-to-shoulder distance an estimate for the head length beyond the shoulder joint and an estimate of the rump length beyond the hip joint to get a total estimate of animal body length.

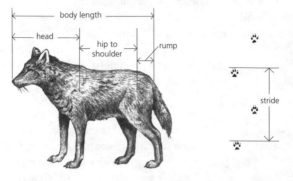

estimating mammal length from stride

Speed also modifies gait patterns in trails. There are three rules governing how pattern changes as speed changes:

1. As speed increases, the hind foot lands farther forward than the front footprint on the same side. Conversely, as speed decreases, the hind foot lands relatively farther back in relation to the front footprint.
2. As speed increases, stride increases.
3. As speed increases, straddle usually decreases.

walk
(slower)

amble
(faster)

Speed changes are easily observed in quadrupedal walk and trot trail patterns. As speed increases, the hind footprint registers in front of the front print. This faster version of a walk is called an *amble*. There is no name for the faster version of a trot. When the animal slows to the point that the hind feet are registering behind the front prints, the animal may be stalking something. Trots are

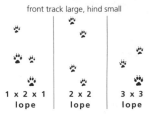

front track large, hind small

1 x 2 x 1
lope

2 x 2
lope

3 x 3
lope

separated from walks by having a stride two or more times greater than the estimated hip-to-shoulder distance of an animal.

A slow version of the gallop is also recognizable. When a gallop slows to the point that one or more hind feet register behind the leading edge of the frontmost footprint in a group pattern, the gait is called a *lope*. The gait is still a gallop, it's just a slow gallop.

Trail measurements

The terms *stride, group, intergroup,* and *straddle* describe the size of an animal trail. The *stride* is measured from the point where a foot touches the ground surface to where the same point of the same foot next touches the surface, and consists of one group and one intergroup measurement. The *group* consists of all four footprints (two fronts, two hinds, two lefts, two rights), while the *intergroup* is the distance between groups. Gait patterns take their name from the configuration of the group. The stride provides an indication of size in a walking animal and an indication of relative speed for other gaits (see pages xvii and xviii).

The *straddle* indicates the width of the trail and is measured from the outside rightmost pad of the outside right footprint of a group to the outside leftmost pad footprint of the same group. The outside edges of the trail are used because the inside of footprints overlap for many carnivore species.

Stride, group, and intergroup are all measured parallel to the trail, while the straddle is measured at right angles to the trail. Select a straight section of trail on level ground to measure. The slightest curve in the trail will distort the straddle measurement.

Glossary of terms

amble: a fast *walk* in which the hind footprint registers anterior to the front footprint. See illustration on page xviii.

asymmetrical: not symmetrical, that is, one side is not a mirror image of the opposite side.

bound: a *gait* in which both hind feet strike the ground at the same time, side by side. If the front feet also land side by side, the motion is said to be a *full bound*. A *half bound* occurs when one front foot strikes the ground in front of the other. See illustration on page xvi.

clout: term used to refer to toe 3 or toe 4 of the hoof. See illustration on page xxiv.

convergent toes: Toes 2 and 4 of ducks, geese, and swans, which bend toward the *foot axis,* especially at the tips. Compare to *divergent toes.*

cord: See *scat shape.*

cough pellet: remnants of bones and hair coughed up by many bird species after feeding on prey.

dewclaw: toe that over evolutionary time has become reduced in size and raised on the leg, away from the other toes. For example, toe 1 in dogs and toes 2 and 5 in deer.

diagnostic: providing certain identification of an animal or its sign.

digitigrade: walking on the tips of the toes. Dogs and cats, for example, are digitigrade. Tracks left by digitigrades rarely show a *sole.* Compare *plantigrade.*

digit: one of the toes of an animal.

digital pad: See *pad.*

distal webbing: See *webbing.*

divergent toes: Toes that are straight or turn out from the *foot axis* at the tips, specifically toes 2 and 4 of sea gulls. Compare to *convergent toes.*

foot axis: imaginary line down the center of the foot. It runs between toes 3 and 4 in deer and their relatives, and down toe 3 of other mammals. In birds, the foot axis also runs down toe 3.

fringe: webbing attached to a single toe. May have a smooth edge, known as a *simple fringe* or *simple lobe,* or it may be wavy, in which case it is said to have *indented lobes.*

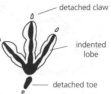

detached claw

indented lobe

detached toe

full bound: See *bound.*

gait: term for the type(s) of movement an animal uses when moving. Examples of gaits include *walk, amble, trot, bound,* and *gallop.* Gaits are defined by the mechanics of body movement, not by speed.

gallop: a *gait* in which hind feet move around the front feet and (usually) strike the ground in front of the front feet. Galloping forms distinct *group* patterns (two fronts, two hinds, two lefts, two rights) separated by an intergroup distance from the next set of four feet. Gallops fall into two basic patterns: Z-shaped and C-shaped.

group: a subunit of a *stride* including four footprints (two fronts and two hinds, and two lefts and two rights). The measure of the group plus the intergroup equals the measure of the stride.

half bound: See *bound.*

heel: portion of foot or track to the rear of digital and interdigital *pads.* In mammals, may be covered with hair, naked (without hair), or have one or more proximal pads. In reptiles and amphibians, may be textured with *tubercles.*

hop: synonymous with *bound,* often used in reference to *gaits* of rodents and rabbits.

indented lobe: See *fringe.*

interdigital pad: See *pad.*

length: of a *track,* the distance from front of toe *pads* to back of the interdigital pads, measured parallel to the *foot axis.* In mammal tracks, does not include claws. In bird tracks, does not include toe 1, but includes claws if they are attached and indistinguishable from toe pad.

line of travel: imaginary line on the ground over which the center of gravity of an animal passes.

lobe: See *fringe.*

lope: a slow *gallop,* in which at least one hind foot registers behind a front foot in a group of four footprints. See illustration on page xix.

mesial webbing: See *webbing.*

minimum outline: See pages xiii–xiv for extended discussion.

nipple-dimple: See *scat shape.*

outer toe angle: in birds, the angle between toes 2 and 4. In perching birds less than 90° and in shorebirds greater than 120°.

oval: See *scat shape.*

pad: hard, callus-like structure on the sole of an animal's foot. Each toe may have a digital pad. One or more interdigital pads are located directly to the rear of the toes, and one or more proximal pads may be located directly to the rear of the interdigital pads. In deer and their relatives, there is a single pad separated from the *wall* by the *subunguinis.* In birds, a metatarsal pad may occur directly under the leg bone.

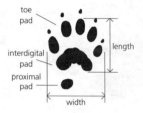

plantigrade: walking on the soles of the foot. Raccoons, bears, and humans, for example, are plantigrade. The *sole* of the foot usually shows in the footprint. Compare *digitigrade.*

pronk: a *gait* in which all four feet strike the ground simultaneously and directly below the body. The *group* pattern shows two front footprints ahead of the two hind prints. Also called a *stot.* See illustration on page xvii.

proximal pad: See *pad.*

proximal webbing: See *webbing.*

rotatory gallop: a type of *gallop* which tends to form a C-shaped *group* pattern. See illustration on page xvi.

run: a *gait* used when moving only on two legs. It differs from a *walk* in having a longer *stride.*

scat shape: *Cords* are long pieces of scat, typically four to ten times longer than the width. Ends may be blunt or tapered. *Ovals* are pieces of scat typically two to four times longer than wide and

tapered at both ends. A *"nipple-dimple"*–shaped scat
pellet has a point at one end and a depression at the
other. See chart on page xii.

simple fringe, simple lobe: See *fringe*.

sole: bottom of an animal's foot. It may be covered with
hair, naked (without hair), and may have one or more
pads on it.

stot: See *pronk*.

straddle: the distance
from the right edge of
the rightmost *pad* to
the leftmost edge of
the leftmost pad in a
trail. Measured at right
angles to the *line of
travel*.

stride: The distance
from the point where a
foot touches the
ground to the point where
the same same foot touches the ground again.
Measured parallel to the *line of travel*. One
stride is equal to a *group* plus an intergroup
measurement.

subunguinis: the soft material under the nails
of humans. In deer and their relatives, refers
specifically to the soft material between the
pad and *wall*.

symmetrical: having two sides, one the mirror image of the other
side.

toe pad: See *pad*.

track: refers to an individual footprint. Some measurable
characteristics include *length* and *width*.

track pattern: the gross visual image of the pattern of footprints
on the ground. A repeating pattern of two prints separated from
the next two is called "two-by" and written 2 x 2. Prints may also
show patterns of 3 x 3, 4 x 4, and 1 x 2 x 1. These patterns are
made during a *gallop* or a *bound*. A few of these patterns are
illustrated on page xix.

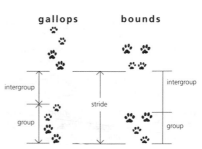

stot

gallops   bounds

trail: a series of footprints and associated sign that marks the passage of an animal. Some measurable characteristics include *stride* and *straddle*.

transverse gallop: a type of *gallop* which tends to form a "Z-shaped" *group* pattern. See illustration on page xvi.

trot: a *gait* in which evenly spaced footprints alternate on right and left sides of the *line of travel*. Hind footprint registers on top of front. As speed increases, hind moves forward of front. Same patterns as a *walk*, but longer *stride*. May be done with body turned to side. See illustration on page xvii.

fast
trot

tubercle: rough pinhead-sized protuberance on the *sole* of the foot of a reptile or amphibian.

unguinis: hard material forming nails in humans, hoof walls in deer and their relatives, and claws in other mammals. Composed of hair pasted together by body glues.

walk: a *gait* where evenly spaced footprints alternate on right and left sides of the *line of travel*. Hind footprint registers on top of front. As speed increases, hind moves forward of front. See illustrations on pages xvi and xviii.

wall: hard material around the edge of each clout of a hoof. Technically the *unguinis*, which also forms human nails and animal claws.

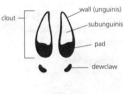

webbing: thin membrane stretched between toes of animals. The webbing may be near the tips of the toes *(distal)*, about midway to the toe tips *(mesial)*, or attached at the base *(proximal)*. A membrane attached to only one toe is called a *fringe*.

width: of a *track*, the greatest distance from the right side of the *pads* of a foot to the left side, whether the greatest distance is across the toes or palm pads. Measured perpendicular to the *foot axis*. In bird tracks, includes claws if they are attached and indistinguishable from toe pad.

How to use *Scats and Tracks*

Scats and Tracks was designed for easy use in the field. The gray bars found on the edges of the pages of the track accounts will help you measure scat diameter and footprint size; each of these bars is keyed to the average size of the sign in question. A ruler is provided on the back cover. Below, we provide the background knowledge that every tracker should be familiar with before going to the field or using this book. Please take some time to study this material.

Illustrations

Illustrator Todd Telander applied his great ability to my collection of plaster casts, photographs, and slides, "drawing" on my experience to produce the most up-to-date and accurate illustrations possible. These drawings—made from the best specimens in a collection of thousands—represent the culmination of decades of tracking experience and are far more accurate than the tracker usually finds in tracking books. The tracks you find on the ground may not have as much detail or be as clear, but it is better to have an excellent drawing to compare to an imperfect track than to have to compare a track to a drawing lacking critical details.

How to use the track accounts

The track accounts in this guide have been grouped by similar footprint characteristics. Each track account represents a single species or a group of species with similar track characteristics. Each account is presented across a two-page spread, and is conveniently divided into sections as discussed below.

A brief listing of visual characteristics used to identify an animal begins each track account, appearing beneath the common and scientific names of the species. These descriptions are general, and great variability of pattern can exist among animals in the field. We recommend consulting appropriate field identification guides.

Track: A concise description of key points of footprints, to be used for identification. The accompanying track illustrations are not at actual size, but, unless otherwise noted, actual (average) length of the footprint is shown as a bar on the right side of the right-hand page. Average width is shown as a bar on the bottom of the right-hand page. In the field, place the appropriate measurement bar next to the track to compare size. To take a numerical measurement, use the ruler printed on the back cover of the book.

The tracks illustrated are all from right feet, except in the entries for birds, where both feet are pictured. Numerical measurements are given in the form *length* x *width*. Note that measurements of mammal tracks do not include claws, that measurements of bird tracks include claws but do not include toe 1, and that measurements generally do not include parts of the foot which may show irregularly in a given species (e.g., heels in the hind feet of some rodent species).

Trail: The average size of the stride of the most commonly used gait or gaits is given. Other common characteristic gaits, if any, are discussed. See *track pattern* in the Glossary of Terms on page xxiii. For more information on gaits in tracking, see my *Field Guide to Mammal Tracking in North America*. Gaits are displayed up the right side of the right-hand page. If the common gait is a walk or trot, however, it may not be illustrated, since all walking and trotting patterns consist of right-left alternating patterns.

Scat: A description of scat supplements the drawing. Average scat width is shown as a bar up the side of the left-hand page. In the field, place the appropriate measurement bar next to the scat to compare sizes. To take a numerical measurement, use the ruler printed on the back cover of the book. Numerical measurements of scat are given under the illustrations in the form *length* x *width*. In cases of small scat, only width is given; thus, a single measurement always indicates diameter.

Habitat: To aid in locating and differentiating tracks, the animal's habitat preferences are listed.

Similar species: Clues are provided to help differentiate an animal's tracks from similar tracks of other species. With these clues, identification should be possible.

Other sign: Other sign of animals, besides tracks and scat, are listed or illustrated to help with identification, and simply to provide more information on animal lives.

In addition, a distribution map is provided with each account. This gives a generalized picture of where in the Pacific Coast region an animal may be found. Animals that require specific habitats will of course not be evenly distributed through the shown range.

To make the best use of this guide, carry it with you into the field. When you come across an unfamiliar track or trail, open the book to the appropriate track account and place the page alongside the track for immediate on-site comparison.

Visual key to tracks

This simple key includes birds, reptiles, amphibians, and mammals. It is arranged by the number of toes that show in a good footprint, ranging from two toes to five toes. Those animals that show four toes in the front print and five toes in the hind are listed between four- and five-toed animals.

Deer and Relatives (pp. 130–141)

Two toes form hard, cloven hoof. Dewclaws may show in deep print.

Birds without Webbed Feet (pp. 30–45)

Three toes facing forward, often a fourth toe facing backward. Claws may be detached from toes.

Birds with Webbed Feet (pp. 12–29)

Three toes facing forward, often a fourth toe facing backward. Claws may be detached from toes. Webbing between two or more toes.

Wolves, Dogs, and Relatives (pp. 50–59)

Four toes in front and hind prints. Claws usually present and detached. Single anterior lobe on interdigital pad.

Cougars, Cats and Relatives (pp. 60–65)

Four toes in front and hind prints. Claws usually absent. Double anterior lobe on interdigital pad.

Rabbits and Relatives (pp. 92–99)

Four toes in front and hind footprint. An exceptionally clear print may show a fifth inner toe in the front footprint. Pads lacking, bottom of foot covered with hair. Long hopping heel in hind print.

Rodents (pp. 100–129)

Most have four toes in front prints and five in hind. Beaver has five toes in front print. Front toes show a 1-2-1 grouping, hind show a 1-3-1 grouping. Long hopping heel in hind print.

Salamanders (p. 2)

Four toes in front print, five toes in hind. Trail wide, often with a tail drag.

Toads (p. 6)

Four toes in front print, five toes in hind. Front print faces center of trail. Mesial webbing in hind print. Tubercles may show on front and hind prints.

Frogs (p. 4)

Four toes in front print, five toes in hind. Long, slender toes. Front print faces center of trail. Distal webbing in hind print.

Raccoons and Relatives (pp. 70–73)

Five toes in front and hind prints. Toes often round or bulbous at ends. May have long, slender toes.

Weasels and Relatives (pp. 74–91)

Five toes in front and hind prints, though the little toe (on inside of foot) may not show. Toes in a 1-3-1 grouping. Interdigital pad is chevron-shaped. Plantigrade hind foot.

Bears (pp. 66–69)

Five toes in front and hind prints, though the little toe (on inside of foot) may not show. Toes evenly spaced. Plantigrade hind foot.

Lizards (p. 10)

Five toes in front and hind prints. Toes long and slender. Claws may be detached. Tail drag often present in trail.

Snakes (p. 8)

Series of side-to-side trail undulations.

Scats
and
Tracks
of the
Pacific Coast

Tiger Salamander
Ambystoma tigrinum

Hot dog–sized salamander, up to 9 in (23 cm) long. Moist, smooth skin. Body brown to black to dark green, with yellow spots or streaks. Tubercles on underside of foot. The only salamander of the high mountains.

Track: Four toes on front foot (often only three show), and five toes on hind foot. The outline of the foot may not show, just toe prints. Even in a clear print, tubercles rarely show.

Trail: Walking stride is about 3 in (7.5 cm). Trail has a wide straddle relative to stride, and may show oscillating belly and tail drag marks.

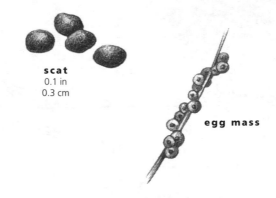

scat
0.1 in
0.3 cm

egg mass

Scat: Soft, pea-sized black masses with some hint of oval shape.

Habitat: Quiet waters around lakes, ponds, and streams in grassland meadow areas and forests. Found to 9,200 ft (2,760 m).

Similar species: Differs from lizards by wider, oscillating tail drag and by having only four toes on front foot.

Other sign: Eggs in egg masses are attached individually to underwater plant stems.

front
0.6 x 0.3 in
1.5 x 0.8 cm

hind
0.8 x 0.6 in
2 x 1.5 cm

amble

FRONT TRACK LENGTH

FRONT TRACK WIDTH

Bullfrog
Rana catesbeiana

Softball-sized frog, 4–8
in (10–20 cm) long.
Brownish green to
brown, becoming
light green on head.
Legs banded with
dark brown to green;
small spots on back.
Fold of skin around eye
and large exposed eardrum.

Track: Four toes on front foot and five on hind. Front feet face in. Three hind toes face in, remaining two face forward or out. Webbing, found only on hind feet, is distal, extending most of the way out to the toe tips. In a clear track, a male's toe 2 ("thumb") on front foot appears thicker at base.

Trail: Hopping stride is 24 in (60 cm). May easily hop 72 in (180 cm).

scat
1.5 x 0.4 in
3.8 x 1 cm

egg mass in water

Scat: Brown to black, with slightly tapered ends.

Habitat: Permanent and (usually) quiet water with dense growth of aquatic plants, especially cattails, in plains, woodlands, chaparral, forest, and desert.

Similar species: Differs from toads by more webbing between toes, lack of palm tubercles on front feet, and by hopping more and at longer distances.

Other sign: Deposits a globular egg mass.

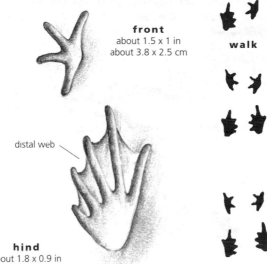

front
about 1.5 x 1 in
about 3.8 x 2.5 cm

walk

distal web

hind
about 1.8 x 0.9 in
about 4.5 x 2.3 cm

hop

FRONT TRACK LENGTH

FRONT TRACK WIDTH

Boreal Toad
Bufo boreas

Baseball-sized toad, up to 5 in (12.5 cm) long. Body is light brown to gray to green, with warty skin and dark spots. A white line runs down the back. Female larger than male. Subspecies of northern  part of the range, *B.b. boreas* is darker with darker blotches. Southern subspecies, the California toad *(B.b. halophilus)*, is less dark, with larger eyes and head.

Track: Four toes on front foot and five on hind. Front feet face in. Two tubercles on heel of front foot. Three hind toes face in, one forward, and one out. Two tubercles may show on the heel of the hind foot, and can be confused with toes. Webbing, found only on hind feet, extends at most halfway out to toe tips.

scat
1 x 0.3 in
2.5 x 0.8 cm

egg mass

toad imprint in mud

Trail: Walking stride is about 3 in (7.5 cm). Hopping stride generally less than 1 ft (0.3 m).

Scat: Dark brown to black. Long cord, up to five times longer than wide. Sometimes contains insect parts.

Habitat: Lakes, ponds, beaver ponds.

Similar species: Differs from frogs by presence of tubercles on front heels. Hind foot is narrower than frog. Walks and uses short hops more than the usually long-hopping frog.

Other sign: Long strings of egg masses on bottom and floating among vegetation.

walk

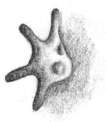

front
0.9 x 0.6 in
2.3 x 1.5 cm

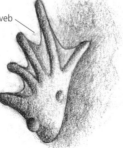

mesial web

hind
1.1 x 0.9 in
2.8 x 2.3 cm

hop

FRONT TRACK LENGTH

FRONT TRACK WIDTH

Western Rattlesnake
Crotalis viridus oreganus

A large snake, up to 5 ft (1.5 m), with rattle at end of tail. Triangular head, elliptical pupils, and keeled (ridged) scales. Body color varies widely, brown to green to black, but is generally similar to local ground color. Back has irregularly shaped brown to black blotches with light border. Light-colored stripe from eye to back of mouth. More than two scales above lip and between nostrils.

Track: No footprint to describe.

Trail: Varies from 1–4 in (2.5–10 cm) in width. Characterized by side-to-side undulations. The *period,* the distance from one curve to the next, varies according to the age and speed of the snake. Surface material is usually pushed up at the outside of each curve. Gait is either a side-to-side undulation or, on loose sand, sidewinding.

Scat: Black or brown cord, with constrictions and undulations. White nitrogenous material often attached.

scat
4 x 0.4 in
10 x 1 cm

shed skin

Habitat: Wide variety of habitats, from coast to above tree line. Ledge and rock outcrops provide cover and nesting. May den in mammal burrows or caves.

Similar species: Rattlesnakes cannot be separated from other snakes by their trail. One rattlesnake species, the sidewinder *(C. cerastes)*, uses the sidewinding movement almost exclusively.

Other sign: Look for shed skins.

lateral undulatory

sidewinding

trail

Short-horned Lizard

Phrynosoma douglassi

Roughly the size of a calling card; body and tail less than 4 in (10 cm) long. Body relatively broad, with short horns projecting from back of head. A single row of fringe scales along edge of body. Body mottled gray to brown to tan, closely matching local terrain colors.

Track: Five relatively long, thin toes on front and hind feet. Hind heel is relatively long. Claws may show.

Trail: Trotting stride is 3 in (7.5 cm). Hind feet mostly register on top of front feet. Relatively wide straddle. Relatively straight tail drag and often a wider body drag.

Scat: Brown pellets three to six times longer than wide. May be tapered at ends. White nitrogenous material may be found on one end.

scat
1.5 x 0.25 in
3.8 x 0.6 cm

SCAT WIDTH

Habitat: Determined by presence of fine, loose soil interspersed with firm, sandy or rocky terrain. Found in prairies and open woodlands, from plains high into mountains.

Similar species: Differs from salamanders by having five narrow toes on front feet and relatively straight tail drag.

Other sign: Scuff marks in loose sand where the lizard buries itself for camouflage.

detached claw

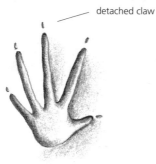

front
about 0.8 x 0.6 in
about 2 x 1.5 cm

hind
about 1 x 0.6 in
about 2.5 x 1.5 cm

amble

FRONT TRACK LENGTH

FRONT TRACK WIDTH

White Pelican
Pelecanus erythrorhynchos

Large aquatic bird, average length more than 60 in (150 cm), with a wingspan of more than 8 ft (2.4 m). White with black primary wing feathers. Large bill is yellow to orange.

Track: Four long, slender toes. Toe 1 offset to side of track. Feet *totipalmate,* with webbing between all four toes. Webbing distal and slightly convex between toes. Claws attached.

Trail: Walking stride averages 16 in (40 cm). Toes turn inward.

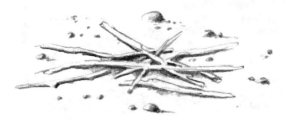

ground nest

Scat: Shapeless, brownish white mass.

Habitat: Lakes, marshes, and bays. During summer, found in freshwater lakes; in winter, in salt water.

Similar species: Differs from all web-footed birds except cormorant by being totipalmate. Differs from cormorant by having attached claws.

Other sign: Nests on ground in large island colonies.

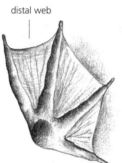

distal web

totipalmate foot

feet
5.7 x 5 in
14.3 x 12.5 cm

walk

TRACK LENGTH

TRACK WIDTH

Double-crested Cormorant
Phalacrocorax auritus

Large aquatic bird, average length
more than 32 in (80 cm), with a
wingspan of more than 4.3 ft
(132 cm). Dark-colored body
with orange throat patch.
Crest of two white
feathers behind
eye, which may
be difficult to
see.

Track: Four long, slender toes. Toe 1 offset to side of track. Toe 4 is longest. Feet
totipalmate, with webbing between all four
toes. Webbing distal and slightly convex
between toes. Claws detached.

Trail: Walking stride is about 10 in (25 cm).
Walks awkwardly on land, with a short stride
for its size. Toes turn inward.

ground nest

Scat: Shapeless, nearly liquid white mass.

Habitat: Saltwater islands, bays, and cliffs. Freshwater lakes, ponds, and swamps.

Similar species: Differs from all web-footed birds except pelican by being totipalmate. Differs from pelican by having detached claws.

Other sign: Nests in colonies on ground or in trees. Acidic scat kills trees and ground vegetation.

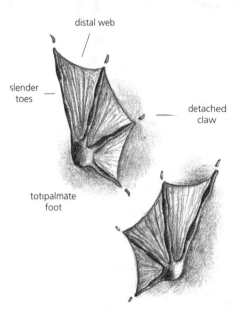

distal web

slender toes

detached claw

totipalmate foot

feet
up to 5.2 x 4.8 in
up to 13 x 12 cm

walk

HALF TRACK LENGTH

HALF TRACK WIDTH

Great Blue Heron

Ardea herodias

Large wading bird, average length 45 in (113 cm). Male and female similar in overall appearance: gray-blue body, with white neck and yellow beak. Black crown extends on feathers off rear of head.

Track: Four toes, toes 2–4 pointing forward. Small proximal web between toes 3 and 4. Footprint is asymmetrical, with toe 1 set to inside of foot axis (drawn through toe 3). Toe 1 is about 1.5 in (3.8 cm); toe 2 is longer than 1, though shorter than 3 and 4. On hard ground, metatarsal pad may not show (that is, toes may appear unconnected).

Trail: Walking stride about 20 in (50 cm). Trail is fairly straight and feet point forward.

cough pellet

nest

rookery

Scat: Semiliquid, predominantly white. Solid cords of scat vary from 2–3 in (5–7.5 cm) in length, and contain fish, frogs, salamanders, and even small rodents. Ground beneath nests becomes coated with droppings.

Habitat: Frequents backwater eddies along riverbanks and shallow edges of lakes.

Similar species: Differs from other shore-edge tracks by large size and asymmetrical placement of toes.

Other sign: Large colonies of nests high in trees. Undigested material may be coughed up as pellets.

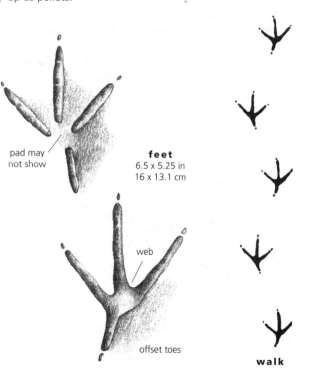

pad may
not show

feet
6.5 x 5.25 in
16 x 13.1 cm

web

offset toes

walk

HALF TRACK LENGTH

HALF TRACK WIDTH

Sandhill Crane
Grus canadensis

Large bird, average length 39 in (98 cm). Appearance of males and females similar: grayish, with red crown on head, and white cheeks and chin.

Track: Four toes, toes 2–4 showing. Outside toes opposed by nearly 180 degrees. Toe 3 is longer than 2 and 4. Small proximal web between toes 2 and 3 rarely shows. Claws usually attached to toes, though claw of toe 1 rarely shows. Feet point forward.

Trail: Walking stride about 24 in (60 cm). Often runs, extending its stride. Tracks have a narrow straddle, being nearly in line with one another.

Scat: Similar to, but smaller than, Canada goose. Brown in color, with some vegetation. Can contain bones of small mammals, reptiles, and amphibians.

scat
2.5 x 0.3 in
6.3 x 0.8 cm

Habitat: Meadows, marshes, grasslands, and fields.

Similar species: Differs from ducks, geese, swans, and herons by having only small proximal web. Differs from large raptors by lacking toe 1.

Other sign: Listen for its rattling call, which suggests to some what dinosaurs may have sounded like.

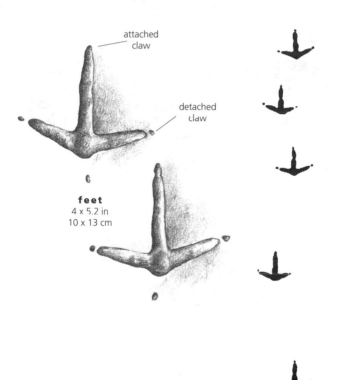

attached claw

detached claw

feet
4 x 5.2 in
10 x 13 cm

walk

HALF TRACK LENGTH

HALF TRACK WIDTH

Canada Goose
Branta canadensis

Medium-sized aquatic bird, average length 30 in (75 cm). Considerable size variation among subspecies. Black head and neck, with a white chin band. Back is olive brown. Male and female similarly colored.

Track: Four toes. Toes 2–4, which point forward, usually register. Toe 1 points rearward and only occasionally shows. Distal webbing between toes 2, 3, and 4. Toes 2 and 4 tend to converge slightly near tips. Claws are broad, blunt, and usually attached to toes. Feet turn in.

Trail: Walking stride is about 12 in (30 cm).

scat
3 x 0.4 in
7.5 x 1 cm

Scat: Cord, five to eight times longer than wide. Often greenish and coated with white nitrogenous deposits. As long as 3.5 in (8.8 cm).

Habitat: Ponds, lakes, marshes, streams, and rivers.

Similar species: Larger than most ducks and smaller than swans. Differs from pelican and cormorant by lacking webbing between toes 1 and 2. Larger than gulls, and differing from them by having convergent toes and distal webbing.

Other sign: Nests on ground, sometimes on cliff ledges, and in abandoned heron and raptor nests. Eggs larger than chicken eggs.

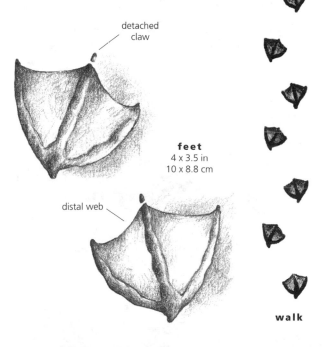

detached claw

distal web

feet
4 x 3.5 in
10 x 8.8 cm

walk

TRACK LENGTH

TRACK WIDTH

Lesser Scaup
Aythya affinis

Aquatic bird, average length 16 in (40 cm). Male with dark head iridescing purple and green. Dark, gray-black body with white sides. Small bill with a small black tip. Female is brown with white at base of beak.

Track: Four toes. Toes 2–4 point forward. Toe 1 points rearward and may not show. Distal webbing between toes 2, 3, and 4. Webbing concave between toes. Toes 2 and 4 tend to converge near tips. Claws are broad, blunt, and attached. Feet turn inward.

Trail: Walking stride is about 12 in (30 cm).

Scat: Pencil-sized cords, four to eight times longer than wide. Often greenish and coated with white nitrogenous deposits.

scat
1.5 x 0.25 in
3.8 x 0.6 cm

Habitat: A duck of ocean bays, estuaries, and freshwater lakes during the winter, it breeds in small bodies of water such as ponds, small lakes, and marshes.

Similar species: Differs from geese and swans by smaller size. Differs from pelicans and cormorants by lacking webbing between toes 1 and 2. Differs from gulls by having convergent toes.

Other sign: Nest is lined with down and placed in a hollow in the grass.

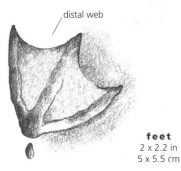

distal web

feet
2 x 2.2 in
5 x 5.5 cm

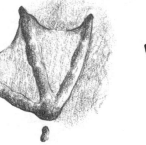

walk

TRACK LENGTH

TRACK WIDTH

Coot
Fulica americana

Medium-sized aquatic bird, average length 15 in (38 cm). Slate-black body, with white beak extending into small brown forehead shield.

Track: Four toes showing, toes 2–4 pointing forward. Toe 1 angles inward. Toes 2, 3, and 4 have fringe of webbing with indented lobes. Long, pointed claws, especially those on toe 1, may be separated from toes.

Trail: Walking stride 10 in (25 cm). Tends to wander when walking. Foot axis is aligned parallel to line of travel.

Scat: White liquid.

Habitat: Freshwater lakes and ponds having shallow water where reeds and rushes grow.

Similar species: Differs from all other aquatic birds by the indented lobes on each toe.

Other sign: Floating nest built from cattails, sedges, and rushes, rising several inches above the water.

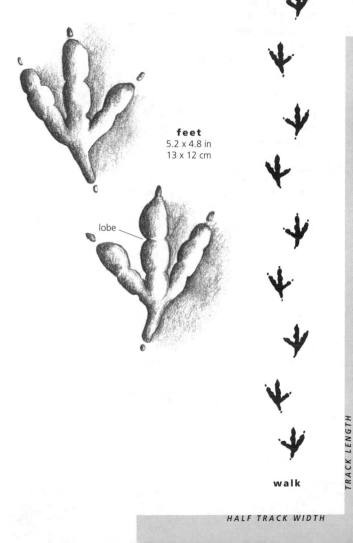

feet
5.2 x 4.8 in
13 x 12 cm

lobe

walk

TRACK LENGTH

American Avocet
Recurvirostra americana

Tall, slender aquatic bird,
average length 18 in (45 cm).
Black-and-white
patterning is striking.
Neck is gray in winter, reddish
during breeding. Distinctive
slender bill curves upward. Long,
slender legs.

Track: Four toes, though toe 1 usually does not register. Outer toes
spread widely. Mesial, concave webbing. Toe
3 extends well beyond the webbing. Claws
attached.

Trail: Walking stride 7 in (18 cm). Toe 3
parallel to line of travel.

Scat: Small and semiliquid. Browns, green,
and white mixed.

nest in grass with twigs

Habitat: Mud flats along marshes, lakes (especially alkaline lakes), ponds, and—in winter—coastal bays.

Similar species: Mesial webbing and long toe 3 separate avocet from other birds with webbed feet.

Other sign: Nests in sparsely vegetated areas of gravel or dry mud flats. Little material incorporated into nest.

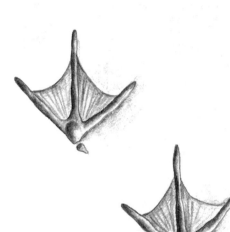

may not show ———————

feet
2.4 x 2.9 in
6 x 7.3 in

walk

TRACK LENGTH

TRACK WIDTH

Herring gull
Larus argentatus

**Large gull, average
length 25 in (63 cm).
Pale gray back, white
head. Tips of primary
feathers black. Bill is
yellow with red spot.
Legs are pink.**

Track: Four toes. Toes 2–4 (forward-point-ing) show. Toe 1 may register only slightly or not show at all. Webbing relatively straight between toes. Toes 2 and 3 tend to diverge, especially at the tips.

Trail: Walking stride is about 13 in (33 cm). Feet turn slightly inward.

Scat: Semiliquid. Primarily white, with indistinguishable contents.

cough pellet

Habitat: Along coast and on inland lakes and rivers. Nests in colonies on ground or cliffs, usually on islands. Nest is made of grass or seaweed. A scavenger, the herring gull is also found at dumps.

Similar species: Differs from ducks, swans, and geese by having divergent toes. Smaller than swans and geese. Differs from coot by having webbing between toes.

Other sign: Cough pellets containing bones, fish scales, urchin parts, and garbage. Cracks mussel shells by dropping onto rocks from high in the air, leaving fragments of the shells.

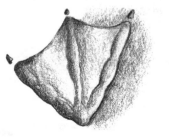

toes 2 and 4 diverge

feet
3.5 x 4 in
8.8 x 10 cm

walk

Eagles
various species

Large birds, average length 35 in (90 cm), with wingspans of 80 in (200 cm). Brown bodies. Adult golden eagle *(Aquila chrysaetos)* has golden feathers over head and neck. Adult bald eagle *(Haliaeetus leucocephalus)* has white head, neck, and tail feathers.

Bald eagle
Haliaeetus leucocephalus

Track: Four wide, robust toes. Toes 2–4 point forward. Lacks webbing and metatarsal pad. Claws are long, sharp, and not attached to the toe print.

Trail: Walking stride about 18 in (45 cm). Golden eagle will run after prey on the ground.

Scat: Semiliquid, primarily white with some brown intermixed.

Habitat: Golden eagle is found in mountainous areas, and hunts over open country. Bald eagle is usually found near lakes and rivers.

cough pellet

urine stain on rock

Similar species: Larger than hawks. Differ from owls by having three toes pointing forward. Differ from geese and swans by lacking webbing. Differ from herons and cranes by having symmetrical feet.

Other sign: Cough pellets may be 5 x 1.5 in (12.5 x 3.8 cm). Nests may be 6 ft (1.8 m) in diameter.

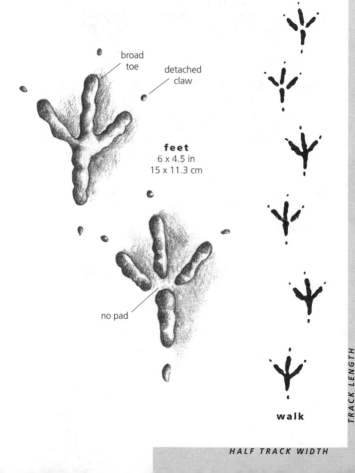

broad toe

detached claw

feet
6 x 4.5 in
15 x 11.3 cm

no pad

walk

TRACK LENGTH

HALF TRACK WIDTH

Grouse

Dendragapus species

Blue grouse
D. obscurus

Size comparable to a chicken, 18 in (45 cm) in length. Spruce grouse *(D. canadensis)* is slightly smaller than blue grouse *(D. obscurus)*. Male blue grouse is speckled gray, black, and white, with yellow eye combs. Male spruce grouse is speckled brown, black, and white, with yellow or red eye combs. Males of both species have dark throat. Females are uniformly mottled brown.

Track: Four toes, with toes 2–4 pointing forward. Toe 1, relatively short, may not show. Toes are relatively wide and lack webbing. Feet point forward to slightly inward. In a clear print, a narrow fringe of scales may show around toes. In winter, feathers on feet show.

Trail: Walking stride is about 9.5 in (24 cm).

Scat: Light to dark brown, sometimes with white nitrogenous covering. Content includes buds, berries, and sawdust. In winter, deposited in snow nest in large mass of 50 or so scats.

scat
1.5 x 0.25 in
3.8 x 0.6 cm

SCAT WIDTH

Habitat: Coniferous forest to the upper timberline.

Similar species: Differ from other forest birds by wide, robust toe size and short toe 1. Grouse trails can be differentiated from those of other forest birds by their short strides and wide straddles.

Other sign: Fly into or burrow under the snow to roost. Tunnel to nest makes a sharp turn, perhaps to confuse predators.

broad toe

feet
2.7 x 2.25 in
6.8 x 5.6 cm

walk

TRACK LENGTH

TRACK WIDTH

California Quail
Callipepla californica

Small, chicken-like bird, average length 10 in (25 cm). Gray-and-brown body, with short, black feather plume on head. White chest scales. Black-and-white pattern on face.

Track: Four toes. Toes 2–4 point forward and slightly outward. Toes 3 and 4 nearly equal in length. Toe 1 detached, but usually registers. When it does, foot length is 2 in (5 cm). Toes relatively wide; lack webbing. Claws attached.

Trail: Walking stride 8–10 in (20–25 cm). Feet point slightly inward.

Scat: Long, thin cord, light to dark brown, occasionally with white nitrogenous covering. Quail's diet of dry vegetation causes scat texture to resemble sawdust. When dry, may break into small fragments.

scat
up to 0.6 x 0.1 in
up to 1.5 x 0.3 cm

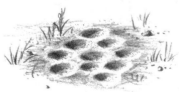

ground roost

SCAT WIDTH

Habitat: Prefers edges of chaparral, woodlands, shrublands, parks, and farms.

Similar species: Differs from grouse by having less robust tracks, narrower toes, and toe 2's tending to be shorter than toes 3 and 4. Tracks are clearer than grouse, especially in winter, as quail lacks toe feathers. Toes broader than those of other ground-dwelling birds. Lack of webbing separates tracks from aquatic birds.

Other sign: Look for dust bath depressions along trails. Ground roosts form a circle of depressions where each bird's tail points into center.

broad toe

feet
1.6 x 1.7 in
4 x 4.3 cm

walk

TRACK LENGTH

TRACK WIDTH

Turkey
Meleagris gallopavo

Large, ground-dwelling
bird. Males average 45
in (113 cm) and females
35 in (88 cm) in length.
Smaller and more slender
than the domesticated
"Thanksgiving" turkey.
Male has a dark brown
to black body, with
white stripes on flight
feather; his tail feathers are tipped with brownish white.
Color of female's feathers is similar but dull. Male also has
red *wattles*, folds of skin hanging from the chin.

Track: Four broad, robust toes. Toes 2–4 face
forward. Hind toe (toe 1) only occasionally
registers; when it does, it registers in a straight
line with toe 4. Only the claw or tip of toe 1
registers. Metatarsal pad present, though it
may be unattached to toes. Claws narrow and
usually attached to toe.

Trail: Walking stride 15 in (38 cm). Foot axis
may vary, pointing into the line of travel or turning slightly
out.

scat
3 x 0.5 in
7.5 x 1.3 cm

SCAT WIDTH

tracks with scratch marks

Scat: Solid scat is long, up to 3 in (7.5 cm), narrow, and brown with white nitrogenous material on ends. Also produces a soft scat that piles in a shapeless mass on ground and is brown to green and white in color.

Habitat: Open forest and shrubland, in trees with lateral branches for roosting at night.

Similar species: Differs from other birds by wide, robust toes. Tracks larger than other ground-dwelling birds. Lacks webbing of ducks and certain other aquatic birds. Separated from eagles by presence (usually) of metatarsal pad. Toes 2 and 4 point forward to a greater degree than those of crane.

Other sign: Scratches on ground where turkey digs for seeds, acorns, nuts, and insects.

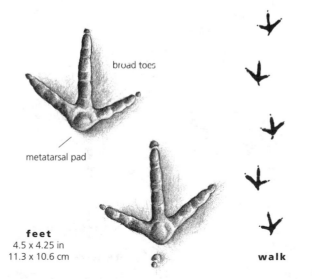

broad toes

metatarsal pad

feet
4.5 x 4.25 in
11.3 x 10.6 cm

walk

TRACK LENGTH

HALF TRACK WIDTH

Owls
various species

Considerable variation in length, from the saw-whet owl *(Aegolius acadicus)*, 8 in (20 cm), to the short-eared owl *(Asio flammeus)*, 15 in (38 cm), to the great gray owl *(Strix nebulosa)*, 25 in (63 cm). All species have immobile eyes offset by facial disks of feathers. Great variability in appearance between species. Typical body colors are grays, browns, and reddish browns.

Short-eared owl
Asio flammeus

Track: Four broad toes, with two paired and facing forward. Toe 4 position is not fixed and may face back or out. Lack webbing and metatarsal pads. Claws long and detached from footprint. Tracks of great horned owl *(Bubo virginianus)* illustrated.

Asio flammeus

Trail: Walking stride varies considerably among species, from 3 in (7.5 cm) to 10 in (25 cm).

cough pellet

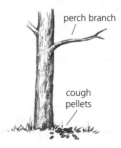

perch branch

cough pellets

perch with pellets

Scat: Semiliquid, primarily white.

Habitat: Forested areas. Some species, such as barn owls, will readily use human structures.

Similar species: Differ from most birds in toes 2 and 3 being paired, nearly parallel, and pointing forward. Differ from woodpeckers by toes being wide and robust, and by toes 1 and 4 being much shorter than toes 2 and 3.

Other sign: Cough pellets below a roost. Diameter of cough pellets ranges from 0.25–1 in (0.6–2.5 cm) and is directly related to the size of the owl. Pellets are shiny and black when new but turn gray with age.

detached claw

feet
2.5 x 2 in
6.3 x 5 cm

walk

Northern Flicker
Colaptes auratus

Medium-sized woodpecker, slightly larger than the American robin, average length 12 in (30 cm). Male has brown-barred back, black chest, white rump, red or black whisker stripe, and is red or orange under wings. Female lacks whisker stripe.

Track: Four toes, with two parallel and pointing forward. Toes 1 and 4 point backward and are not equal in length. Strong, rigid tail feathers may show on ground.

Trail: Walking stride is about 3 in (7.5 cm). Hopping stride is about 4 in (10 cm).

Scat: Cord, about four times longer than wide. Often contains undigested parts of insects.

Habitat: Open woodlands, cottonwood bottoms, and around towns.

Similar species: Differs from three-toed woodpecker by presence of toe 1. Differs from other birds its size by having two toes pointing forward.

scat
1 x .25 in
2.5 x 0.6 cm

SCAT WIDTH

Other sign: Excavates and nests in tree cavities. Does not add bedding material to cavity nest.

tree with beak holes

toes point forward

feet
1.75 x 0.75 in
4.4 x 1.9 cm

walk

TRACK LENGTH

TRACK WIDTH

Black-billed Magpie
Pica pica

Black and iridescent
green body, wings, and
unusually long tail.
Average length about
20 in (50 cm). Belly is
white. Beak is black.

Track: Four medium-wide toes, three facing
forward. Toe 1 nearly as long as toes 2, 3,
and 4. Lacks webbing and metatarsal pad.
Claws long and detached from footprint.

Trail: Walking stride is about 6 in (15 cm).

Scat: Semiliquid, brown with white intermixed.

cough pellet

Habitat: Lower mountains, in open woodlands, thickets, along stream edges. Often found near human habitation.

Similar species: Differs from songbirds by larger size and relatively wide toes. Smaller than crows and ravens.

Other sign: Caches food in trees and under bark. Cough pellet is 1.25 x 0.4 in (3.1 x 1 cm).

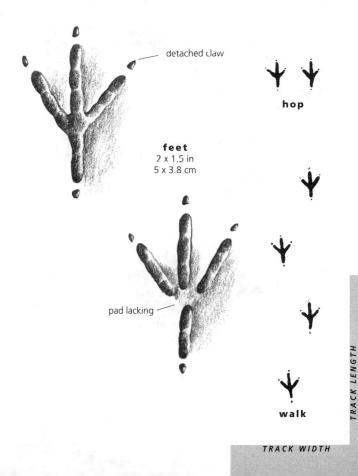

detached claw

feet
2 x 1.5 in
5 x 3.8 cm

pad lacking

hop

walk

Common Raven
Corvus corax

Large black bird, average
length 24 in (60 cm).
Beak heavy. Tail is wedge-
shaped in flight. Size
varies considerably,
though male is larger than
female.

Track: Four toes, toes 2–4 facing forward.
Length of toe 1 nearly equals toes 2, 3, and
4. Lacks webbing and metatarsal pad. Claws
long and detached from footprint.

Trail: Walking stride varies considerably, but
is about 20 in (50 cm). Also runs, with a longer
stride.

Scat: Semiliquid, brown, black, and white.
Often oily. May contain remnants of its omnivorous diet.

Habitat: Mountains, especially where carcasses of deer and elk
can be found, and at garbage dumps. Will beg food from
picnickers.

cough pellet

Similar species: Track and trail of the common crow are diminutive versions of the raven's. Lacks the paired forward facing toes of owls. Lacks the long toe 1 of hawks. Smaller than eagles.

Other sign: Cough pellets up to 3 x 0.5 in (7.5 x 1.3 cm). Caches food in forks of trees and, often, by burying.

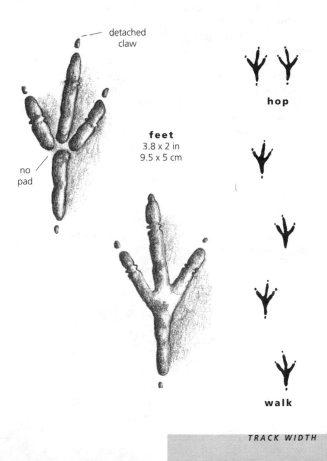

detached claw

feet
3.8 x 2 in
9.5 x 5 cm

no pad

hop

walk

Opossum
Didelphis marsupialis

The size of a large domestic cat, but more stout, nearly hairless, and with a round, rat-like tail. Weight varies from 8–14 lb (3.5–6.5 kg). Face whitish, with thin, black-edged ears. Body is whitish with gray and black hairs interspersed.

Track: Five toes. Hind print is distinctive, with an opposable (like the human thumb) inside toe protruding sideways from other toes. Outside toe is slightly separated from middle three toes. Front footprint is wider than long and shows long toes that widen slightly toward the end.

Trail: Walking stride 18 in (45 cm). Walking trail often reflects slow movement, with hind footprint registering behind the front. Trail is sloppy and footprints seldom register directly. Tail drag often shows. Walking pattern occasionally similar to that of the raccoon, where the hind footprint registers beside the front footprint.

scat shape is highly variable

scat
4 x 0.5 in
10 x 1.3 cm

SCAT WIDTH

Scat: Highly variable shape and size and lack of distinctive form reflect highly variable, omnivorous diet. Single scat may be up to 4 in (10 cm) long.

Habitat: Prefers riparian areas, woodlands, and farmyards. Habitat is not restricted by diet, as the opossum will eat small mammals, birds, eggs, reptiles, amphibians, fish, carrion, fruit, and any garbage it can find.

Similar species: Trail may be confused with those of muskrats, woodrats, and domestic rats when a tail drag is present. However, the distinctive hind footprint and large size of the opossum identify its trail.

Other sign: Dens in logs, stumps, rock crevices, and dens of other animals.

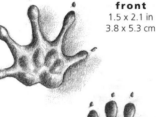

front
1.5 x 2.1 in
3.8 x 5.3 cm

hind
2.2 x 1.9 in
5.5 x 4.8 cm

opposable toe

walk

FRONT TRACK LENGTH

FRONT TRACK WIDTH

Shrews

various species

Smaller than mice, less than 0.25 oz (7 g). Long, pointed nose. Minute eyes and ears. Color brown to black, with gray to white belly. Eat mostly insects.

Masked shrew
Sorex cinereus

Track: Five slender toes are present on front and hind feet. In clear prints, four interdigital and two proximal pads may be seen.

Trail: Hopping stride seldom more than 2 in (5 cm). The group of tracks is less than 1 in (2.5 cm) long. Seldom is the stride more than three times the group.

Scat: Usually small pellets with tapered ends.

Habitat: Found everywhere from deserts to alpine areas. Look for tracks in wet, fine mud of riparian areas or in snow along logs or the edges of buildings. Wood piles and leaf litter make good homes.

————— tapered ends

scat
0.2 x 0.1 in
0.5 x 0.3 cm

insect remains

SCAT WIDTH

Similar species: Differ from mice and voles by having five toes on front foot.

Other sign: After eating, leave body parts from insects they have killed. Often burrow just below the surface of the snow, opening tunnels that partially collapse and expose their route. Trails in the snow radiate from holes like spokes of a wheel.

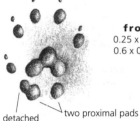

front
0.25 x 0.2 in
0.6 x 0.5 cm

detached
interdigital pad

two proximal pads

six pads

furred heel, not included
in track measurement

hind
0.3 x 0.2 in
0.8 x 0.5 cm

bound

FRONT TRACK LENGTH

FRONT TRACK WIDTH

Red Fox
Vulpes vulpes

Border collie–
sized, 6–15 lb
(3–7 kg).
Reddish
yellow, with
black stockings
and a white tip
on the tail.
Regional color phases include silver, black, cross, and bluish
gray. Long, pointed ears and elongate, pointed muzzle.

Track: Claws prominent. A ridge of callus
present across interdigital pad. One lobe on
the leading edge of the interdigital pad. Inside
toe slightly larger than outside. Front foot
larger than hind.

Trail: Trotting stride averages 32 in (80 cm).
Typically uses a trotting gait and, occasionally,
a 2 x 2 trot with body turned to the side.
Walks more than coyote, especially in shrubs.

Scat: Often has tapered tail. Composition varies. Mouse or rabbit
fur, berries, and insects are common. Bird feathers and plant
remains often present.

Habitat: Found in a variety of habitats from brush to croplands
to mixed hard- and softwood forest. Prefers edges, where hunting

scat
2 x 0.6 in
5 x 1.5 cm

log

SCAT WIDTH

for small mammals is good. Also found in urban areas, where cover is available during the daytime. Not found in dense forests.

Similar species: Differs from other canids by having a ridge of callus on the interdigital pad. Track tends to be larger than gray fox, and usually shows claws. Differs from bobcat in having only one lobe on the interdigital pad and claws (usually) showing.

Other sign: Multiple dens are used each season. Often digs own den. A given den may be used for several years. Look for small bones around den entrance. Scat has a diagnostic musky odor, produced by a musk gland on the top of the tail. Learn to identify this unique "foxy" odor. Foxes tightrope-walk on narrow logs.

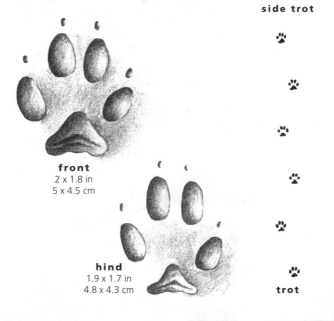

side trot

front
2 x 1.8 in
5 x 4.5 cm

hind
1.9 x 1.7 in
4.8 x 4.3 cm

trot

FRONT TRACK LENGTH

FRONT TRACK WIDTH

Gray Fox
Urocyon cinereoargenteus

Smaller than a border collie, 8–11 lb (4–5 kg). Body color is pepper-and-salt. A black stripe runs down the back and upper side of tail. Sides are reddish. Tip of tail is black. Long, pointed ears and elongate, pointed muzzle.

Track: Small for a canid, somewhat broad and therefore somewhat catlike. Claws, rarely present in track, are very small and sharp, giving the gray fox the ability to climb trees like a cat. Front foot larger than hind.

Trail: Generally a trot. Trotting stride averages 24 in (60 cm). Walks more than coyote.

Scat: Often has tapered tail. Composition varies, as the gray fox is opportunistic when feeding. Rabbit fur is most common, followed by fur of other small mammals, berries, and insects. Plant remains are often present.

scat
2 x 0.6 in
5 x 1.5 cm

Habitat: Prefers a mixture of fields and woods. More often found in woodlands than is red fox. Early stage woodlands are preferred, with considerable activity in riparian habitats.

Similar species: Smaller than coyote and wolf. Lacks the ridge of callus on the interdigital pad of the red fox. Differs from coyote in that claws often do not show.

Other sign: Seldom digs dens, but makes use of woodpiles, rock outcrops, hollow trees, and brushpiles. Look for small bones around den entrances.

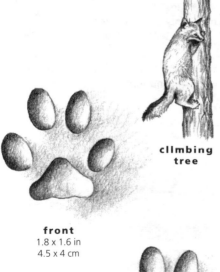

side trot

climbing tree

front
1.8 x 1.6 in
4.5 x 4 cm

hind
1.7 x 1.6 in
4.3 x 4 cm

trot

FRONT TRACK LENGTH

FRONT TRACK WIDTH

Kit Fox
Vulpes macrotis

The size of a domestic cat, 3–5 lb (1.4–2.3 kg), with disproportionately large ears. Body color is pale red washed with gray. Tail has a black tip.

Track: Small for a canid. Claws often do not show. Front foot larger than hind.

Trail: Walking stride 14 in (35 cm). Loping stride 22 in (55 cm). Dainty trail often mistaken for that of a cat. Details of footprint seldom register in sand.

Scat: Usually has a tapered tail. Scat consists mostly of small mammals and insects, but occasionally birds and reptiles.

scat
2 x 0.6 in
5 x 1.5 cm

SCAT WIDTH

Habitat: Found in sand habitats of the desert or plains where vegetation is sparse and short.

Similar species: Smaller than coyote, whose claws show better. Lacks the ridge of callus on the interdigital pad of the red fox. Tracks may be smaller than gray fox, although distinction may be difficult, but the sand habitat is a good clue.

Other sign: Dens in burrows in the ground, where it hides during the day.

front
1.7 x 1.5 in
4.3 x 3.8 cm

hind
1.3 x 1.2 in
3.3 x 3 cm

lope

walk

FRONT TRACK LENGTH

FRONT TRACK WIDTH

Coyote
Canis latrans

Collie-sized canid, 20–25 lb (9–11 kg). Male larger than female. Color varies from completely gray to tan to rust. Long, pointed ears and long, narrow muzzle.

Track: Claws usually present. One lobe on the leading edge of the interdigital pad. Inside toe slightly larger than outside. Front foot larger than hind.

Trail: Trotting stride averages 39 in (98 cm). Often uses a trot with body turned to the side, leaving a 2 x 2 track pattern. Often lopes, leaving a C-shaped pattern.

Scat: Varies from pure black animal protein to mostly hair with some bones. Tips tapered into long tails.

Habitat: An animal of the open brush country, the coyote digs its den on exposed hilltops or ridges with a view of surrounding area. Where persecuted, may den in a more secluded location.

Similar species: Even adult track is smaller than that of a wolf pup. Track may overlap in size with red fox, but lacks callus

scat
3 x 0.6 in
7.5 x 1.5 cm

SCAT WIDTH

ridge of red fox. Track larger than gray fox, and usually shows claws. Differs from bobcat by showing claws and by having one lobe on leading edge of interdigital pad.

Other sign: Marks territory with urine and scat piles. Scat pile locations may be used repeatedly. Uses feet to scratch near scat piles, spreading odor from scat and foot glands to identify territory.

**scratch
marks
near scat
pile**

lope

front
2.5 x 2.35 in
6.3 x 5.8 cm

hind
2.25 x 1.9 in
5.6 x 4.8 cm

side trot

FRONT TRACK LENGTH

FRONT TRACK WIDTH

Gray Wolf
Canis lupus

Larger than a German
shepherd, 110–130 lb
(50–60 kg). Male larger
than female. Color varies
from completely black to
gray to white. Short,
rounded ears and short,
wide, blocky muzzle.

Track: Track diameter of a grapefruit. Claws usually present; one lobe on leading edge of interdigital pad. Inside toe slightly larger than outside. Front foot larger than hind.

Trail: Trotting stride averages 62 in (155 cm). Often uses a C-shaped gallop or a trot with the body turned to the side, leaving a 2 x 2 pattern.

Scat: Varies from pure black, toothpaste-like animal protein to mostly hair with some bones. Tips tapered into long tails.

Habitat: Found in all habitats. Tends to use cover when possible, moving in forest or at forest-meadow edge.

Similar species: Track larger than other canids. At 60 days of age, track larger than adult coyote's. Differs from mountain lion by having one lobe on the leading edge of the interdigital pad and usually showing claws. Differs from wolverine and bear by

scat
4 x 1.25 in
10 x 3.2 cm

SCAT WIDTH

having only four toes, with the large toe on the inside.

Other sign: The alpha wolf, dominant member of the pack, marks its territory by urinating on raised objects along the trail. Blood observed during January or February in the female's urine stain may indicate readiness to breed. Scratch marks beside urine stains or scat are territorial markings, and are usually made with hind feet.

urine mark of alpha wolf

side trot

front
4.25 x 4 in
10.6 x 10 cm

hind
3.75 x 3.25 in
9.4 x 8.1 cm

gallop

FRONT TRACK LENGTH

FRONT TRACK WIDTH

Bobcat
Felis rufus

Size of a collie, with male averaging 17 lb (8 kg) and female 13 lb (6 kg). Overall color reddish to yellowish brown, with dark spots or streaks and whitish underside. Ears have tufts at tips. Back of ears and top of tail tip black. Tail is short or "bobbed," about 4 in (10 cm) long.

Track: Front track is round or wider than long. Hind track may be longer than wide. Claw impressions are usually absent. Toes form a slight arc and toe 3 leads. The leading edge of the interdigital pad has two lobes. Inside toe distinctly larger than outside toe.

Trail: Walking stride is about 20 in (50 cm). Usually walks, but bounds with hind feet placed side by side when chasing prey. Winter trails often show random vertical leaps, perhaps signalling that the bobcat has jumped after a flying bird.

Scat: Tends to be constricted and, if dry, separates at constrictions into segments. Ends usually blunt. Dry scat falls apart. Scat from a fresh kill may form a cord of uniform diameter.

broken
constriction

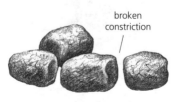

scat
3 x 0.8 in
7.5 x 2 cm

SCAT WIDTH

Habitat: Prefers dense cover of swamps and forests, especially with rocky ledges. Open agricultural land is not used. Rock piles, caves, and high rocky ledges are important for bearing young.

Similar species: Differs from coyote by lacking claws, having two lobes on the leading edge of the interdigital pad, and having toe 3 leading. Substantially smaller than both lion and lynx.

Other sign: Scent marks made by urine, scat, and anal glands. Scrapes dirt or snow over urine and scat. Scratches from rubbing glands are apparent on snow. Caches food by burying.

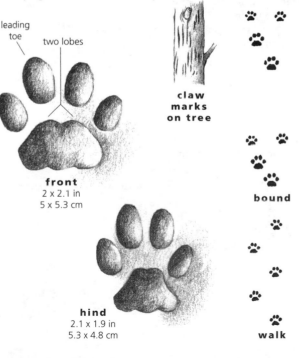

leading toe

two lobes

front
2 x 2.1 in
5 x 5.3 cm

claw marks on tree

hind
2.1 x 1.9 in
5.3 x 4.8 cm

walk

vertical leap from hind feet

bound

walk

FRONT TRACK LENGTH

FRONT TRACK WIDTH

Canada Lynx

Felis lynx

Larger than a collie, with male averaging 22 lb (10 kg) and female 19 lb (9 kg). Very long legs and big feet. Reddish to yellowish brown overall, with dark spots or streaks and whitish underside. Ears have tufts at tips. Tail tip is black on top and bottom. Tail is short or "bobbed," about 4 in (10 cm) long.

Track: Diameter of a softball and indistinct because the feet are mostly covered with hair, and because pads are reduced in size. Feet are large, for better support on snow.

Trail: Walking stride is about 28 in (70 cm). Walking gaits are common, but lynx does trot more than bobcat. Winter trails often show random vertical leaps, perhaps signalling that the lynx has jumped after a flying bird.

Scat: Tends to be constricted and, if dry, separates at constrictions into segments. Ends blunt. Dry scat falls apart. Scat from

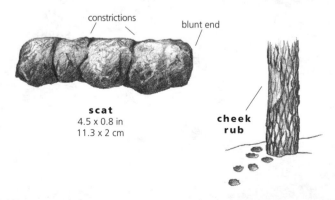

constrictions   blunt end

scat
4.5 x 0.8 in
11.3 x 2 cm

cheek rub

a fresh kill may form a cord of uniform diameter.

Habitat: Found in dense conifer forests interspersed with rocky ledges and downed timber, both of which are used for security and denning. Forest edges, which provide food for the lynx's major prey, snowshoe hare, are critical.

Similar species: Track differs from other felids by being inherently indistinct. Interdigital pad is relatively small when compared to bobcat and mountain lion—check closely.

Other sign: Birth dens occur in hollow logs, stumps, and clumps of timber. Adult lynx does not cover scat. Lynx urinates (scent marks) up to 25 times per mile.

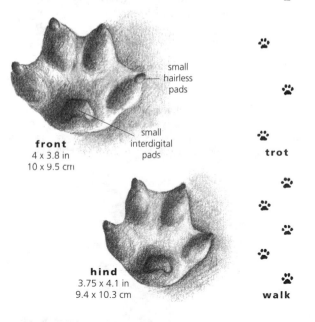

fast trot

vertical
leap from
hind feet

front
4 x 3.8 in
10 x 9.5 cm

small
hairless
pads

small
interdigital
pads

trot

hind
3.75 x 4.1 in
9.4 x 10.3 cm

walk

FRONT TRACK LENGTH

FRONT TRACK WIDTH

Mountain Lion
Puma concolor

Larger than a
German
shepherd, with
male averaging
145 lb (66 kg)
and female
about 120 lb
(54 kg). Color
gray to red, often called "tawny," with whitish underside. Back
of ears and tip of tail black to brown. Tail is more than half the
length of the body. Also called cougar or puma.

Track: Track diameter of a baseball. Front
track round or wider than long, and hind
track longer than wide. Claw impressions are
usually absent. Toes form a slight arc and
toe 3 leads. Leading edge of the interdigital
pad has two lobes. Inside toe distinctly larger.

Trail: Walking stride is about 36 in (90 cm).
Usually walks, but bounds with hind feet
placed side by side when chasing prey.

Scat: Scat from a fresh kill may form a cord of uniform diameter with very slight constrictions; ends usually blunt. As the
carcass a lion is feeding on dries out, the lion's scat tends to
develop constrictions, eventually falling apart when diet becomes
very dry.

scat
4 x 1.25 in
10 x 3.1 cm

Habitat: Habitat is that of its main prey, deer. Open woodlands with rock ledges and grass (for deer) preferred. Often found in riparian zones with trees.

Similar species: Track differs from wolf by the presence of two lobes on the leading edge of the interdigital pad, by having toe 3 leading, and by usually not showing claws. Differs from wolverine and bears by having only four toes and large toe inside.

Other sign: Often buries scat by scraping dirt over it with front feet. Scraped ground material may conceal food caches. Male will rake up basketball-sized patches of brush and urinate on them to mark home range.

bound

scraped ground around scat

two lobes

front
3.5 x 3.6 in
8.8 x 9 cm

hind
3.25 x 3 in
8.1 x 7.5 cm

walk

FRONT TRACK LENGTH

FRONT TRACK WIDTH

Black Bear
Ursus americanus

Calf-sized bear, female averaging 120 lb (54 kg) and male about 300 lb (135 kg). Male grows faster and obtains larger size than female. Color varies from black to brown to blond to red.

Track: Claws on front foot, seldom longer than toes, are usually present. Little toe is set back from rest of toes. Hind print has a large, humanlike heel. Outside toe is larger than others.

Trail: Walking stride 35–40 in (88–100 cm). Usually *ambles,* a fast walk where the hind foot oversteps the front. Gait is pigeon-toed. Lopes in a C-shaped pattern or a side gallop.

Scat: Normally contains vegetation and is sweet-smelling. When feeding on carcasses, scat varies from black to brown, with mostly

animal protein

scat
7 x 1 in
17.8 x 2.5 cm

berry seeds

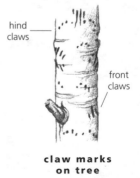

hind claws

front claws

claw marks on tree

hair and some bones. Ants often found in scat. Tips have a short taper or are blunt.

Habitat: Forest, seldom venturing far into wide openings. Thick understory vegetation and abundant food sources are critical.

Similar species: Differs from grizzly bear by smaller size, shorter claw length, and more curved arc of toes. Differs from wolverine by having toes tightly packed and having a wedge-shaped interdigital pad. Differs from lion and wolf by having five toes.

Other sign: Claws trees, rips open logs, digs into ant piles, and turns over rocks and scat as it looks for insects, but seldom digs out roots.

side lope

lope

faint little toe — big toe

front
4.5 x 4 in
11.3 x 10 cm

arch —

hind
7 x 3.5 in
17.8 x 8.8 cm

amble

Grizzly Bear
Ursus arctos horribilis

Large, cow-sized bear, female averaging 350 lb (160 kg) and male about 450 lb (200 kg). Both sexes have hump over shoulders. Color varies from black to brown to blond. Light tips on individual hairs create the grizzled appearance for which grizzlies are named.

Track: Claws on front foot, typically more than 1.5 times longer than toes. Webbing occurs between toes; look carefully. Hind print has a large, humanlike heel. Outside toe larger than others.

Trail: Walking stride 50–60 in (125–150 cm). Usually *ambles,* a fast walk where the hind foot oversteps the front. Gait is pigeon toed. Lopes in a C-shaped pattern or uses a side gallop.

Scat: Normally contains vegetation and is sweet-smelling. When feeding on carcasses, scat varies from black to brown, with mostly hair and some bones. When feeding in alpine areas may contain only parts of moths. Ants often found in scat. Tips have a short taper or are blunt.

mixed vegetation

blunt end

scat
10 x 1.5 in
25 x 3.8 cm

body rub area

Habitat: High forests to alpine tundra meadows. Stays close to cover, foraging at forest-meadow edge.

Similar species: Differs from black bear by flatter arc of toes, longer claws, and webbing. Differs from wolverine by having toes tightly packed and having a wedge-shaped interdigital pad. Differs from wolf and lion by having five toes.

Other sign: Claws trees, rips open logs, digs into ant piles, digs out roots and rodent caches, and turns over rocks and scat as it looks for insects. Rubs body against tree trunks, smoothing bark and leaving hair.

side lope

lope

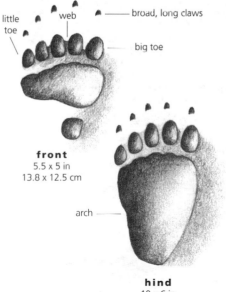

little toe   web   —— broad, long claws

big toe

front
5.5 x 5 in
13.8 x 12.5 cm

arch ——

hind
10 x 6 in
25 x 15 cm

amble

FRONT TRACK LENGTH

HALF FRONT TRACK WIDTH

Ringtail
Bassariscus astutus

Small, rat-sized, with a bushy tail as long as its body. Males average 1.5–2.5 lb (0.7–1.1 kg), with females slightly smaller. Pointed face, large eyes and ears. Tan to gray overall, with some black hairs. Tail has black bands alternating with white to a black tip.

Track: Five toes, round and somewhat bulbous, with an extra proximal pad showing in the front print. Claws are semi-retractile and may not show.

Trail: Bounding stride is 12–16 in (30–40 cm). Uses a relatively slow bound or lope much of the time.

Scat: Usually composed of plant material, but occasionally black animal protein scats are found. Insects and fruits are often present.

scat
2 x 0.4 in
5 x 1 cm

chewed cactus on cliff runway

SCAT WIDTH

Habitat: Found in a variety of habitats from riparian to desert to open woodland to evergreen forest. Rest sites and dens are located in rocks, burrows, brushpiles, and hollow limbs. Not averse to using buildings for nests and dens.

Similar species: Differs from domestic cats, bobcats, and small foxes by having five toes and an extra proximal pad.

Other sign: Runways at the bases of cliffs are used repeatedly and trails often lead to a single rock crevice where the ringtail dens.

lope

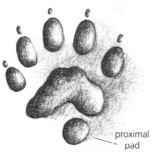

proximal
pad

front
1 x 1 in
2.5 x 2.5 cm

hind
1 x 1 in
2.5 x 2.5 cm

bound

FRONT TRACK LENGTH

FRONT TRACK WIDTH

Raccoon
Procyon lotor

Stocky, smaller than a collie, with broad head and bushy tail. Male averages 18 lb (8 kg) and female 16 lb (7 kg). Gray to black overall, with black rings on the tail and a black mask on a white face.

Track: Five slender toes, slightly bulbous on the ends. Feet resemble small human hands and feet. Hind foot has a long, naked heel.

Trail: Walking stride averages 27 in (68 cm). Roll of hips during walk causes hind foot to register beside the opposite front print. C-shaped gallop is common.

Scat: Highly variable, but often black, even-diameter cord with blunt ends. Often contains crayfish or fruit. Deposited singly or in dung heaps containing scat from perhaps several individuals. May carry a parasite that is fatal to humans. Do not smell scat, and wash hands after touching.

Habitat: River and stream drainages are prime habitats, but storm drains in cities may also provide refuge.

blunt end

scat
3 x 0.75 in
7.5 x 1.9 cm

SCAT WIDTH

Similar species: Differs from bear in having slender toes. Differs from river otter by lack of webbing. Larger than mink.

Other sign: Digs holes in stream banks to get at crayfish. Leaves piles of crayfish skeletons and claws. Digs for worms in lawns.

sign left while fishing for crayfish

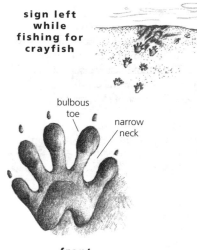

bulbous toe

narrow neck

front
2.5 x 2.5 in
6.3 x 6.3 cm

hind
4 x 2.3 in
10 x 5.8 cm

gallop

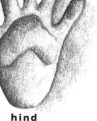

walk

FRONT TRACK LENGTH

FRONT TRACK WIDTH

Weasels
Mustela species

Long-tailed weasel
M. frenata

Three species,
with long,
slender bodies,
varying in size
from a regular to a foot-long hotdog. Pointed, flat skull
with small ears. Males up to twice as large as females. Largest
males weigh about 1 lb (0.5 kg). Overall color is brown, with a
white belly. In winter, northern individuals turn entirely
white. Hairy, slender tail. The small least weasel *(M. nivalis)*
lacks the black tip on the tail found in the ermine
(M. erminea) and the long-tailed weasel *(M. frenata)*.

Track: Wide track. Five toes, in 1-3-1 grouping. Little toe, on inside of foot, often does
not register. Interdigital pad chevron-shaped.
Heel seldom shows. Difficult to distinguish
between species.

Trail: Galloping stride varies from 8–30 in
(20–75 cm). Side-by-side tracks, when ex-
amined closely, show one track slightly in front
of the other—a gallop. In snow, a drag mark may be found
between front and hind prints, sometimes forming a dumbbell
shape.

Scat: Long, slender cord, usually with black, toothpaste-like animal
protein or hair. Cord tends to fold back on itself. Tapered at
both ends.

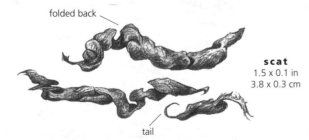

folded back

scat
1.5 x 0.1 in
3.8 x 0.3 cm

tail

SCAT WIDTH

Habitat: Prefer dense, low ground cover to open areas. Found in habitats where their prey, rodents, occur in high densities. Trails often lead from one rodent den to another. Travel in snow and ground burrows of other mammals.

Similar species: Differ from other mustelids by their smaller size and the drag mark commonly located between twin track patterns in the snow.

Other sign: Routes seldom follow a straight line, often having many sharp turns. Scat often deposited on raised objects.

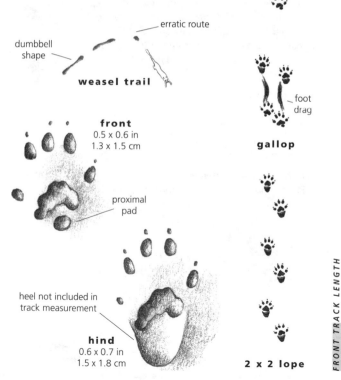

erratic route

dumbbell shape

weasel trail

front
0.5 x 0.6 in
1.3 x 1.5 cm

proximal pad

foot drag

gallop

heel not included in track measurement

hind
0.6 x 0.7 in
1.5 x 1.8 cm

2 x 2 lope

FRONT TRACK LENGTH

Marten
Martes americana

Size of a small domestic cat, but slender, 1–2 lb (0.5–1 kg). Male 20 percent larger than female. Pointed, flat skull with small ears. Overall color golden brown, with orange to yellow chest patch. Edges of ears are white. Hairy, slender tail.

Track: Five toes, in 1-3-1 grouping. Little toe, on the inside of foot, sometimes does not register. Interdigital pad chevron-shaped. Proximal pad may show in front footprint. Heel often shows. Feet well furred in winter, making tracks indistinct.

Trail: Galloping stride averages 22 in (55 cm). Mostly gallops; a variety of 2 x 2, 3 x 3, and 4 x 4 patterns may be found.

Scat: Long, slender cord, tending to fold back on itself. Black or brown in color, occasionally with hair. Tapered at both ends.

Habitat: Old-growth forest, but adaptable to many forest habitats. Prefers mature conifer and mixed forests. Needs tall, hollow, or

scat
2 x 0.25 in
5 x 0.6 cm

folded back

SCAT WIDTH

climbs tree, jumps out

broken trees for denning. Found near its prey, squirrels and red-backed voles.

Similar species: Differs from weasel by its larger size. Lacks the webbed toes of the mink. Also differs from mink by use of terrestrial habitat. Smaller than fisher and occupies areas with deeper snow.

Other sign: Frequently burrows beneath snow and climbs up trees; look for tracks that end at a tree trunk. Scratch marks show where stomach was dragged over objects that protrude from the ground or snow to scent mark.

4 x 4 gallop

proximal pad

front
2.1 x 2 in
5.3 x 5 cm

furred heel, not
included in track
measurement

hind
2.3 x 2.1 in
5.8 x 5.3 cm

2 x 2 lope

FRONT TRACK LENGTH

FRONT TRACK WIDTH

Mink
Mustela vison

Size of a small domestic cat, but slender, 1.5–3.5 lb (0.7–1.5 kg). Male 10 percent larger than female. Pointed, flat skull with small ears. Overall color is dark brown, with white spots on chin and chest. Hairy, slender tail. Webbing occurs between the toes.

Track: Five toes, in 1-3-1 grouping. Little toe, on the inside of foot, sometimes does not register. Webbing shows between toes in tracks; look carefully. Interdigital pad chevron-shaped. Proximal pad may show in front footprint. Heel seldom shows.

Trail: Bounding stride averages 14 in (35 cm). Bounds more than weasels, but a gallop, averaging 20 in (50 cm), is also common.

Scat: Long, slender cord, usually tending to fold back on itself. Black or brown in color, occasionally with hair. Tapered at both ends. Often contains remains of fish or crayfish. May be oily and smell fishy. Fish oil keeps scat composed of fish scales from falling apart until oil evaporates, then scales scatter on the ground.

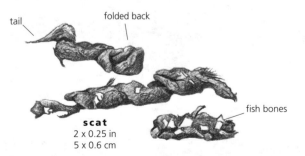

tail

folded back

scat
2 x 0.25 in
5 x 0.6 cm

fish bones

Habitat: River and stream banks. Seldom far from water.

Similar species: Differs from other small mustelids by having more webbing between toes. Larger than weasels. Use of aquatic habitat is an important clue for separation from marten. Tracks and trail much smaller than otter's.

Other sign: Mink make "post offices," repeated scat deposits on logs exposed above water's edge. Strong, musky, almost skunk-like odor from anal scent glands.

fast walk

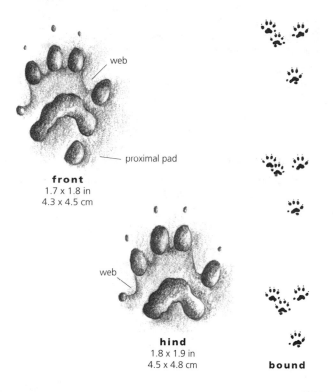

web

proximal pad

front
1.7 x 1.8 in
4.3 x 4.5 cm

web

hind
1.8 x 1.9 in
4.5 x 4.8 cm

bound

FRONT TRACK LENGTH

FRONT TRACK WIDTH

Fisher

Martes pennanti

Larger than a large domestic cat, but slender, 7.5–12 lb (3–5 kg). Male larger than female. Pointed, flat skull with small ears. Color is dark brown. Long bushy tail.

Track: Five toes, in 1-3-1 grouping. Little toe, on the inside of foot, sometimes does not register. Interdigital pad chevron-shaped. Proximal pad may show in front footprint. Heel seldom shows. Claws short. Feet are not well furred, which, in winter, makes toes appear clearly in tracks.

Trail: Galloping stride averages 28 in (70 cm). Mostly gallops, but walking, 3 x 3, 1 x 2 x 1, and 4 x 4 gallop patterns are also common.

Scat: Only mustelid scat that frequently contains porcupine quills. Long, slender cord, usually tending to fold back on itself. Black or brown in color, occasionally with hair. Tapered at both ends.

Habitat: Old-growth forest, especially among conifers and large timber, and in swamp areas. Will use young forest stands following

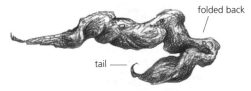

folded back

tail —

scat
3.5 x 0.5 in
8.8 x 1.3 cm

SCAT WIDTH

fire or timber harvest. Avoids open areas without overhead cover, but will travel on roads and trails.

Similar species: Lacks the webbed toes of the mink. Differs from mink by habitat and use of terrestrial sites. Larger than mink and marten and occupies areas of shallower snow. Smaller than wolverine and makes more frequent use of trees for walkways and nests.

Other sign: Porcupine skins turned inside out. Snow trails may reveal frequent trips up trees. Walks on logs to avoid deep snow. Drags stomach over objects that protrude from the ground or snow to scent mark, leaving scratches. Travels on packed trails of snowshoe hare.

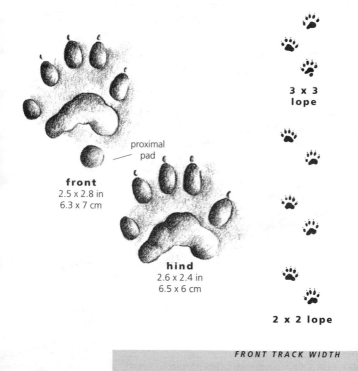

1 x 2 x 1 lope

3 x 3 lope

2 x 2 lope

proximal pad

front
2.5 x 2.8 in
6.3 x 7 cm

hind
2.6 x 2.4 in
6.5 x 6 cm

FRONT TRACK LENGTH

FRONT TRACK WIDTH

Striped Skunk
Mephitis mephitis

Black-and-white
mustelid, size of a
domestic cat, with
triangular head.
Weight varies from
4–10 lb (2–5 kg).

Male is slightly larger than female. Flat, wide, bushy tail with
white hair on top. Long, curved claws for digging.

Track: Half dollar–sized, with long front claws.
Hind track looks like a little human footprint.
Five toes, in 1-3-1 grouping. Little toe, on
the inside of foot, sometimes does not register. Interdigital pad chevron-shaped. Proximal pad often shows. Hairless heel on hind
foot.

Trail: Walking stride averages 12 in (30 cm).
Meanders and stops often when walking, leaving "extra footprints" in trail. Lope may be turned to the side or straight forward.

Scat: Cylindrical with blunt ends. Lacks the long taper and tendency to fold back on itself of other mustelid scat. May be composed entirely of insect parts.

blunt

scat
5 x 0.75 in
12.5 x 1.9 cm

fang puncture

**chewed
eggs**

Habitat: Not habitat-specific. Lives where burrows, cavities, or tunnels are present, including in and around buildings. Presence of insects and small mammals is critical to habitat selection.

Similar species: Differs from other species by having long, wide claws on the front foot. Smaller than badger, with front and hind feet similar in size.

Other sign: Smell of skunk musk identifies nests and burrows. Tears apart nests of small mammals. Bird eggs show four fang punctures around larger hole in shell.

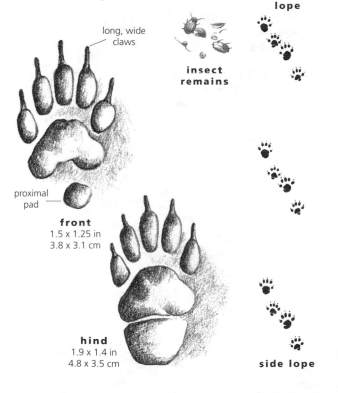

lope

long, wide claws

insect remains

proximal pad

front
1.5 x 1.25 in
3.8 x 3.1 cm

hind
1.9 x 1.4 in
4.8 x 3.5 cm

side lope

Spotted Skunk
Spilogale putorius

Black and white, the size of small domestic cat. Male weighs 1–2 lb (450–900 g), female 0.5–1.25 lb (225–560 g). Distinctive pattern of white spot on forehead, a spot by each ear, four white stripes along each side, and a white tip on tail. Spots and stripes highly variable.

Track: Size of a quarter, with longer claws on front footprint. Five toes, though 1-3-1 grouping is difficult to identify. Little toe, on the inside of foot, may not register. Clear front and hind prints on a hard surface may show a total of six hairless interdigital and proximal pads. Plantigrade heel on hind foot.

Trail: Loping stride is about 12 in (30 cm). Short bounds are very common. Often rambles as it walks, leaving a confused trail with most front and hind prints registering separately.

blunt

scat
1.5 x 0.25 in
3.8 x 0.6 cm

insect remains

SCAT WIDTH

Scat: Cylindrical, with blunt ends. Lacks the long taper and tendency to fold back on itself of other mustelid scat. May be composed of mouse fur, bird feathers, insects, and carrion.

Habitat: Brush, chaparral, and open woodlands, especially along streams and in boulder areas.

Similar species: Distinguished from striped skunk by smaller track size and by presence of multiple foot pads.

Other sign: Nests in burrows beneath rock and wood piles or under buildings.

lope

front
0.9 x 1 in
2.3 x 2.5 cm

heel not included
in measurement

faint pad

hind
1.25 x 0.9 in
3.1 x 2.3 cm

heel not included
in measurement

side lope

FRONT TRACK LENGTH

FRONT TRACK WIDTH

River Otter
Lutra canadensis

Body and tail form a 4-foot-long cylinder that tapers to a hairy, pointed tail. Weight varies from 10–30 lb (5–14 kg). Male slightly larger than female. Overall color a rich, dark brown, with silver-brown belly. Webbed toes on front and hind feet.

Track: Large webbed foot is diagnostic, but look closely because webbing may be difficult to see. Hind foot is very wide. Five toes, in 1-3-1 grouping. Little toe, on the inside of foot, sometimes does not register. Interdigital pad chevron-shaped. Proximal pad often shows. Hairless heel on hind foot.

Trail: Walking stride averages 19 in (48 cm). Loping stride averages 32 in (80 cm). Loping gait patterns are usually turned to the side.

Scat: Usually contains fish remains, including scales and vertebrae. The texture is oily and the smell fishy. Fish oil keeps scat composed of fish scales from falling apart. Scat decomposes as oil evaporates, eventually falling into a pile of scales.

fish parts

scat
5 x 1 in
12.5 x 2.5 cm

SCAT WIDTH

Habitat: River and stream beds. Lives and nests in bank burrows, but may also nest in log jams. In spring, travels overland, often several miles from water sources.

Similar species: Differs from other species by webbing and wide hind foot.

Other sign: Loose dirt banks show where otters have rolled to dry off. Rolls around tufts of grass, twisting them into scent posts. Travels by sliding down banks and along level snow and over ice-covered lakes.

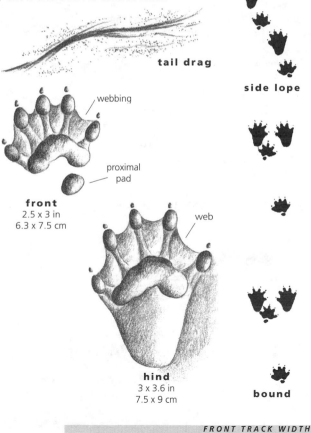

tail drag

side lope

webbing

proximal pad

front
2.5 x 3 in
6.3 x 7.5 cm

web

hind
3 x 3.6 in
7.5 x 9 cm

bound

FRONT TRACK LENGTH

FRONT TRACK WIDTH

Wolverine
Gulo gulo

Body like a badger's but heavier, up to 35 lb (16 kg). Male larger than female. Head broad, rounded, and flat. Color varies from overall dark brown with light blond side stripes to nearly all blond. Short tail.

Track: Track diameter of a baseball. Five toes, in 1-3-1 grouping. Little toe, on the inside of foot, sometimes does not register. Interdigital pad chevron-shaped. Proximal pad and heel often show. Distinct winter tracks because feet are not well furred.

Trail: Galloping stride averages 35 in (88 cm). Mostly 2 x 2 and 3 x 3 gallop patterns.

Scat: Long, medium-diameter cord, occasionally folding back on itself. Black or brown, occasionally with hair. Tapered at both ends. Similar to large coyote scat.

Habitat: Not habitat-specific. Wanders widely in all seasons, though often found where there are wintering deer, elk, or moose.

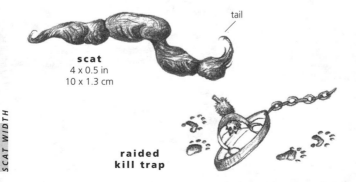

tail

scat
4 x 0.5 in
10 x 1.3 cm

**raided
kill trap**

SCAT WIDTH

Similar species: Larger than mink, marten, and fisher, and only rarely climbs trees. Differs from wolf and lion by having five toes. Differs from bear by having 1-3-1 toe grouping and chevron-shaped interdigital pad.

Other sign: Scavenges on old carcasses, including those of animals caught in kill traps. Revisits sites to dig carcasses from under snow. Drags stomach over objects that protrude from ground or snow to scent mark, leaving scratches. Trails cross large openings in trees and are often found above tree line. Travels on packed trails and roads.

**3 x 3
gallop**

proximal
pad

front
3.7 x 3.8 in
9.3 x 9.5 cm

naked heel

hind
4 x 3.5 in
10 x 8.8 cm

**1 x 2 x 1
gallop**

FRONT TRACK LENGTH

FRONT TRACK WIDTH

Badger
Taxidea taxus

Border collie–
sized, with flat
body, long hair, and
long, shovel-like
claws, about 18 lb
(8 kg). Male 25
percent larger than
female. Color varies from silver-gray to yellowish brown on
back. Belly white. Feet are black or dark brown. White stripe
down nose with black markings on sides of face. Short tail.

Track: Diameter of a golf ball, with long front
claws, nearly as long as rest of footprint. Five
toes, in 1-3-1 grouping. Little toe, on the
inside of foot, sometimes does not register.
Interdigital pad chevron-shaped. Proximal pad
often shows. Front footprint larger than hind.

Trail: Walking stride averages 14 in (35 cm).
Walking is most common, but trotting, with
a stride of 29 in (73 cm), occurs frequently.

Scat: Seldom found because deposited below ground in burrows. Similar to, but smaller than, coyote scat, without tapered
ends.

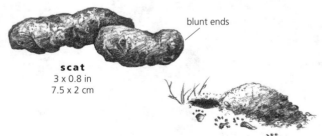

scat
3 x 0.8 in
7.5 x 2 cm

blunt ends

hole with dirt mound

SCAT WIDTH

Habitat: Open grasslands preferred. Areas with large populations of prey, which includes ground squirrels and prairie dogs.

Similar species: Differs from all other species by long claws on front foot and disproportionately small hind foot.

Other sign: Fresh excavations of large amounts of dirt from burrowing rodent holes indicates hunting activity, especially if excavated material includes large clods or rocks. Freshly widened burrow entrances may have a slightly elliptical shape. The presence of coyote and badger tracks together indicates cooperative hunting.

———— long, prominent claws

proximal pad

front
2.5 x 2 in
6.3 x 5 cm

1 x 2 x 1 lope

heel not included in track measurement

hind
1.75 x 1.75 in
4.4 x 4.4 cm

walk

FRONT TRACK LENGTH

FRONT TRACK WIDTH

Brush Rabbit
Sylvilagus bachmani

Small cottontail rabbit with relatively short ears; weighs about 1.5 lb (675 g). Body is brownish, with a small white tuft of a tail. Other species of cottontails are found in the region, but this is the most widespread. Tracks of cottontail *(Sylvilagus)* species are often indistinguishable.

Track: Toes asymmetrical around foot axis. Track indistinct because the foot is completely haired and lacks pads. Claws occasionally register; on hard ground, they may be the only sign of a hopping rabbit. Hind footprint about two and a half times as long as front.

Trail: Hopping stride is about 36 in (90 cm). Most of the time rabbits hop, but walking patterns are occasionally observed.

scat
0.3 in
0.8 cm

chewed branch and bud

Scat: Dry scat is a slightly flattened sphere. Produces a black, semiliquid scat that is usually reingested to utilize remaining nutrients.

Habitat: Thick brush and chaparral interspersed with grass.

Similar species: Differs from jackrabbit and hare by having shorter heels and smaller overall track size.

Other sign: Sharp incisors cut herbaceous vegetation at the height of a sitting rabbit, 4–6 in (10–15 cm). The brush rabbit's nest, known as a *form,* is a shallow depression in earth or grass.

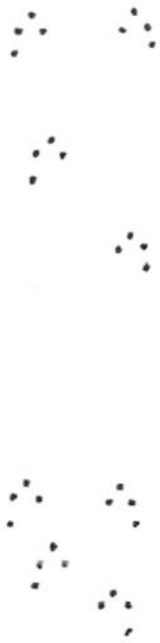

claw

toe position asymmetrical

claws only on hard ground

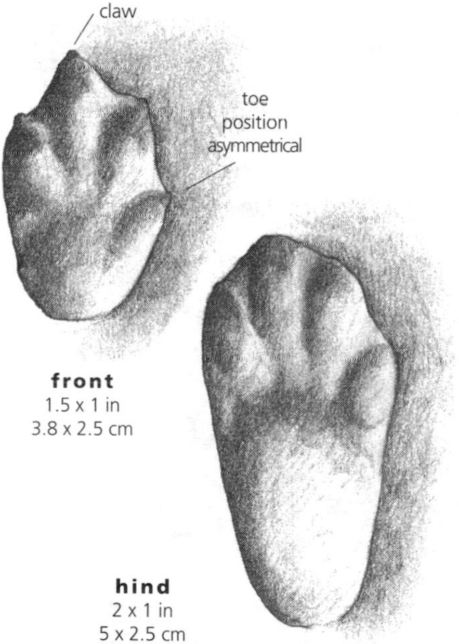

front
1.5 x 1 in
3.8 x 2.5 cm

hind
2 x 1 in
5 x 2.5 cm

hop

FRONT TRACK LENGTH

FRONT TRACK WIDTH

Jackrabbit
Lepus species

Large, slender hare with long—6 in (15 cm)—ears and large feet. Weighs 3–7 lb (1.4–3.2 kg). Body color is brownish gray. Tips of ears, top of tail, and rump are black. White-tailed jackrabbit *(L. townsendii)* of northern areas has a white tail, and may turn white in winter.

Black-tailed jackrabbit
L. californicus

Track: Toes asymmetrical around foot axis. Track indistinct because the foot is completely haired and lacks pads. Claws occasionally register; on hard ground, they may be the only sign of a footprint. Hind footprint about three times longer than front. Footprints of white-tailed jackrabbit are about 10 percent longer.

Trail: Galloping stride may reach 10 feet (3 m). Tends to gallop rather than bound.

Scat: Dry scat is a slightly flattened sphere. Produces a black, semiliquid scat that is usually reingested to utilize remaining nutrients.

scat
0.3 in
0.8 cm

Habitat: Sparsely vegetated open areas of the desert and plains. White-tailed jackrabbit is found from plains grasslands to above tree line in the mountains.

Similar species: Differs from snowshoe hare by narrow width of hind print. Hind track differs from cottontail by greater length.

Other sign: Sharp incisors cleanly cut herbaceous vegetation at the height of a sitting rabbit, 4–6 in (10–15 cm). The jackrabbit's nest, known as a *form,* is a shallow depression, usually located under protective cover.

sharp cut grass

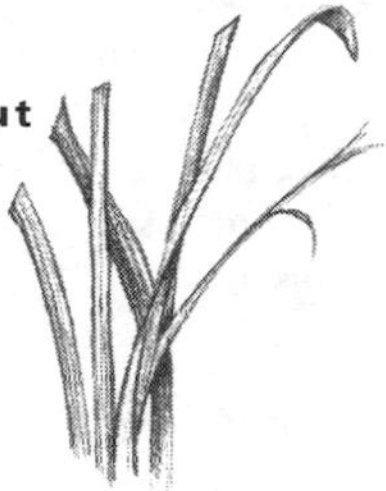

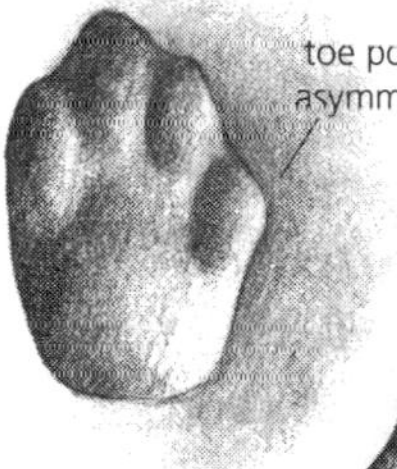

toe position asymmetrical

front
1.5 x 1.2 in
3.8 x 3 cm

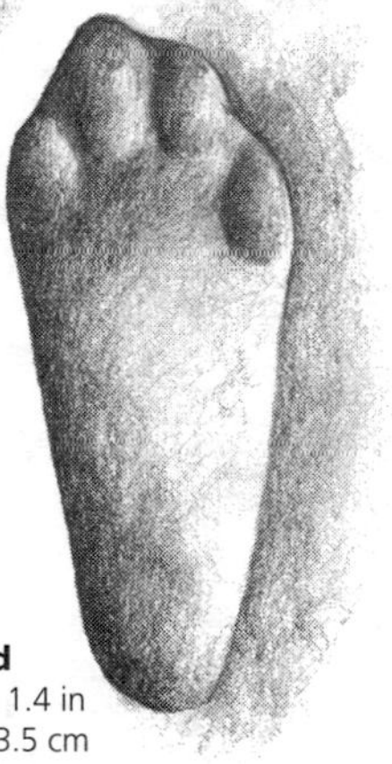

hind
up to 4.8 x 1.4 in
up to 12 x 3.5 cm

gallop

FRONT TRACK LENGTH

FRONT TRACK WIDTH

Snowshoe Hare
Lepus americanus

Medium-sized hare with long ears and feet. Averages about 3 lb (1.4 kg). Body color is rusty to gray brown, turning white in the winter. Ears retain their black tip in winter.

Track: Toes asymmetrical around foot axis. Track indistinct because the foot is completely haired and lacks pads. Hind footprint may be up to two and a half times longer than front. To provide flotation on snow, hind feet are exceptionally wide and toes may splay apart so that width approaches length.

Trail: Hopping stride varies from 3–6 ft (0.9–1.8 m). Tends to hop with paired hind feet.

Scat: Dry scat is a slightly flattened sphere. Produces a black, semiliquid scat that is usually reingested to utilize remaining nutrients.

scat
0.3 in
0.8 cm

chewed branch and cone

SCAT WIDTH

Habitat: High mountains with deep snows. Dense second-growth forest is preferred, but swamps are also used. Forages at forest edge and in small clearings.

Similar species: Track differs from cotton-tail by its large size and from jackrabbit by its relative width.

Other sign: Look for woody plants, including conifers, that have had the tips of branches chewed off. During population highs, hares will strip tree bark and have been observed feeding on carcasses. The snowshoe's nest, a shallow depression known as a *form,* is found under conifer branches or logs.

toe position
asymmetrical

front
1.75 x 1.5 in
4.4 x 3.8 cm

hind
4.5 x 3.75–4.5 in
11.3 x 9.4–11.3 cm

hop

FRONT TRACK LENGTH

FRONT TRACK WIDTH

Pika

Ochotona species

Small—average weight
5 oz (140 g)—rat-sized,
short-legged, nearly
tailless, egg-shaped
member of the rabbit
order (Lagomorpha).
Large ears and
relatively large eyes.
Color gray to
grayish brown. The
collared pika *(O. collaris)* of British Columbia has an
indistinct gray collar on the back of its neck.

Pika
O. princeps

Track: Shows four toes. Only in a very clear
footprint will the minute inside toe on the
front foot be observed. Unlike the rest of the
rabbit order, the pika's track shows toe pads.
The sole is haired.

Trail: Prefers a hop, with a stride of 15 in
(38 cm). Even when moving fast, the stride
is seldom more than three times the group.

Scat: Produces two types of scat. Those most readily found are
nearly spherical and dry. Also produces a black, semiliquid scat
that is usually reingested to utilize remaining nutrients.

scat
0.1 in
0.3 cm

Habitat: Found almost exclusively in the rock and talus fields of high mountains.

Similar species: Differs from chipmunk and other rodents by having only four toes on hind foot. Track is larger than mouse or vole.

Other sign: Marks territory by urinating on prominent rocks, leaving a white, hard stain. Scat may be placed nearby. Stores plants under and around rocks near the center of its territory. These hay piles dry and provide food for the pika during the winter.

hay pile

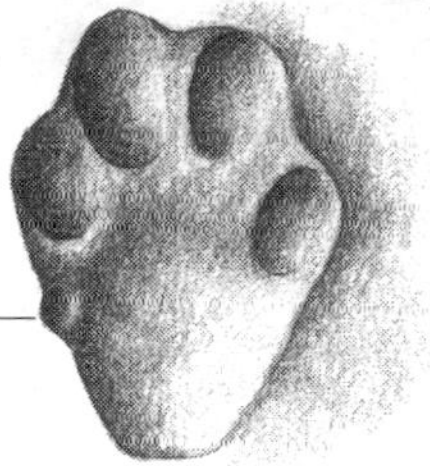

minute inside toe

front
0.75 x 0.6 in
1.9 x 1.5 cm

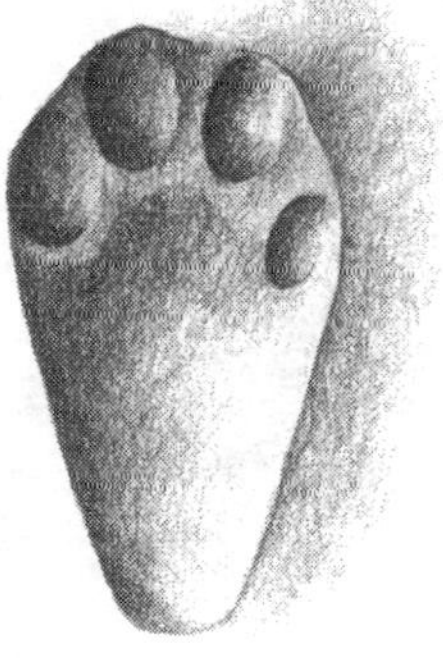

hind
1 x 0.75 in
2.5 x 1.9 cm

hop

FRONT TRACK LENGTH

FRONT TRACK WIDTH

Aplodontia (Mountain Beaver)
Aplodontia rufa

Size of a large guinea pig, 2–3 lb (0.9–1.4 kg). Dark brown and nearly tailless with small, rounded ears and small eyes. The aplodontia is a very primitive rodent that, although called a beaver, is only very distantly related to the true beaver, which is in another rodent family.

Track: Five toes with relatively long, wide claws on each foot. The inside toe of the front foot lacks a claw. Toes in the front print show a 1-4 grouping, toes in the hind a 1-3-1 grouping. The heel of the front foot is square in shape, that of the hind footprint tapered.

Trail: Walking stride 6–8 in (15–20 cm). Hind foot often understeps the front footprint.

Scat: Three to four times longer than wide and often tapered at both ends.

scat
up to 1.6 x 0.4 in
up to 4 x 1 cm

open burrow with hay pile

SCAT WIDTH

Habitat: Moist settings in dense forest. Favors loose soil and plant debris where it can build its burrow systems. Often present in logged areas.

Similar species: Distinguished from other rodents by front foot's inner toe lacking claw. Shape of the footprint is characteristic of this species only.

Other sign: Burrows are 4–8 in (10–20 cm) in diameter and raised ground may show above ground. Burrows often cave in. After snow melt, solid casts of soil and rocks show where aplodontia packed dirt into tunnels in the snow while burrowing during winter. Aplodontia make hay piles to dry ferns and herbaceous plants for nest material and food storage. These are often on logs, not in rock fields, where those of pika can be found.

front
1.2 x 0.8 in
3 x 2 cm

hind
1.8 x 0.9 in
4.5 x 2.3 cm

walk

track illustration based on information presented by Olaus Murie

FRONT TRACK LENGTH

FRONT TRACK WIDTH

Hoary Marmot

Marmota caligata

Size of a large, fat domestic cat, 10–20 lb (4.5–9 kg). Male larger than female. Ears and muzzle are short. Head and shoulders are black and gray. Body is yellowish gray. Feet are black. Brown hairy tail.

Track: Front foot larger than a silver dollar, with four toes in a 1-2-1 grouping. Five toes on hind foot, 1-3-1 grouping. Toes relatively slender. Four joined interdigital pads and two proximal pads on front footprint make the heel appear squarish. In the hind footprint, they give the heel a tapered appearance. Heel is hairless.

Trail: Bounding stride varies from 30–70 in (75–175 cm). A ground dweller, the marmot uses a half bound.

Scat: Wide variety of forms, from oval pellets to long cords, all of which may be tightly stuck together. Sometimes lacks defined shape, being dark and runny when deposited. Deposited in "latrines" or "post offices" on top of prominent rocks and along ledges.

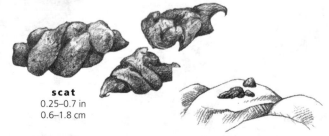

scat
0.25–0.7 in
0.6–1.8 cm

scat on rocks

Habitat: Found high in the mountains, near and above tree line. Uses talus slopes for den sites and refuge, but talus must be near grass meadows for feeding.

Similar species: Largest of the ground squirrels, its track dwarfs those of other squirrels. Track left when drinking at a stream may be distinguished from beaver's by lack of webbing and by having only four toes on front prints. Tracks distinguishable from the yellow-bellied marmot *(M. flaviventris)* of the eastern portions of the Pacific coast states and British Columbia only by their larger size, those of the hoary marmot's being 10 percent or more larger. Distinguished from raccoon by lack of an inner toe on the front foot.

Other sign: Burrow system with multiple openings, though dirt may be excavated through only one of the openings, allowing others to remain hidden.

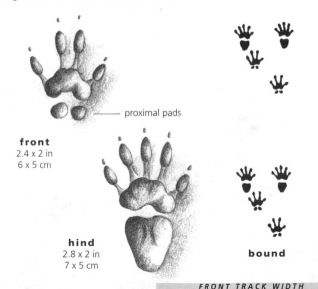

front
2.4 x 2 in
6 x 5 cm

—— proximal pads

hind
2.8 x 2 in
7 x 5 cm

bound

FRONT TRACK LENGTH

FRONT TRACK WIDTH

California Ground Squirrel

Spermophilus beecheyi

Size of a small rat,
1–2 lb (450–900 g).
Body has brownish
fur spotted with
white to tan flecks.
Back and top of rump are
darker in color. Shoulders are
tinted with white. Tail is bushy with
white hair on the edge.

Track: Front print has four toes, with 1-2-1 grouping. Hind has five toes, with 1-3-1 grouping. Toes relatively slender. Front footprint size of a quarter. Hind heel is hairless and may register clearly in track. Long claws may show, especially in front tracks.

Trail: Bounding stride averages 25 in (63 cm). Uses a half bound, characteristic of its terrestrial life style.

Scat: Small, usually unconnected ovals.

scat
0.2 in
0.5 cm

SCAT WIDTH

burrow entrance

Habitat: Rocky areas with low vegetation in grasslands and open woodlands. Not found under dense timber or chaparral.

Similar species: *Spermophilus* species cannot be differentiated from one another by tracks. Habitat and visual identification are necessary. Claws longer and feet smaller than those of tree squirrels. Lack the long claws of prairie dogs. Smaller than marmots.

Other sign: Burrows have many openings; underground portion is long, up to 200 ft (60 m). *Runways,* worn paths indicating repeated use, are found between burrow openings. Stores food in a den and makes a nest of dry vegetation.

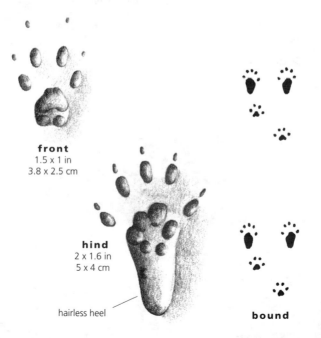

front
1.5 x 1 in
3.8 x 2.5 cm

hind
2 x 1.6 in
5 x 4 cm

hairless heel

bound

FRONT TRACK LENGTH

FRONT TRACK WIDTH

Chipmunk

Tamias species

Least chipmunk
T. minimus

Slightly larger than a large mouse, up to 2 oz (56 g). Reddish fur, with white stripes bordered by black stripes along the sides of the face and body. Haired tail.

Track: Front foot size of a nickel, with four toes in 1-2-1 grouping. Five toes on hind foot, 1-3-1 grouping. Toes relatively slender. Claws short. Hind heel is haired and details are difficult to detect.

Trail: Bounding stride averages 7 in (18 cm). Mostly terrestrial, it usually uses a half bound, though full bounds may be observed in its trails.

Scat: Small, usually unconnected ovals.

Habitat: Varies, but includes coniferous forest and shrubland. Usually found near rocks.

scat
0.1 in
0.3 cm

Similar species: Smaller than ground and tree squirrels. Lacks the long claws of prairie dog and ground squirrel. Smaller than marmot.

Other sign: Seeds and nuts of various plants, chewed open on one side.

front
0.5 x 0.4 in
1.3 x 1 cm

furred heel, not included
in track measurement

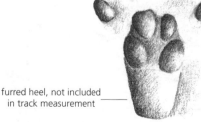

hind
0.7 x 0.6 in
1.8 x 1.5 cm

half bound

FRONT TRACK LENGTH

FRONT TRACK WIDTH

Chickaree

Tamiasciurus douglasii

Small to
medium-sized
tree squirrel,
less than 0.5 lb
(226 g). Body is light
gray with tints of red,
especially on legs. Darker in
winter. In summer, yellowish to orangish belly is separated
from upper body by a black stripe on side.

Track: Front foot size of a quarter, with four
toes in 1-2-1 grouping. Five toes on hind foot,
1-3-1 grouping. Toes relatively slender. Claws
relatively short. Haired hind heel is indistinct
in tracks.

Trail: Bounding stride averages 22 in (56 cm).
Tends to use a full bound, characteristic of
its arboreal life style. (Half bounds indicate a
ground squirrel.)

Scat: Small, shapeless masses to small, usually unconnected ovals.

Habitat: Restricted to boreal or northern coniferous forests.
Infrequently found in deciduous forests.

scat
0.1 in
0.3 cm

**chewed cones
and seed
casings**

Similar species: Larger than chipmunk. Lacks the long claws of prairie dog and ground squirrel. Smaller than marmot. Track slightly smaller than its more eastern relative, *T. hudsonicus,* which is found in Washington and Oregon.

Other sign: Builds twig and leaf nests in branches of trees. Also nests in hollow trees. Leaves piles of cone scales (called *middens*) where it removes scales to get at seeds. Cones are cached deep in the midden for use as winter food.

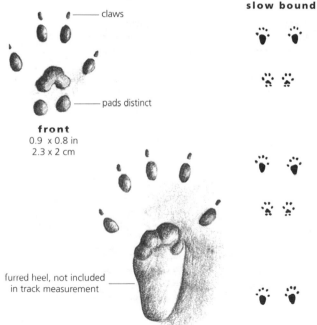

claws

pads distinct

front
0.9 x 0.8 in
2.3 x 2 cm

furred heel, not included in track measurement

hind
0.8 x 0.9 in
2 x 2.3 cm

hind prints on front

slow bound

full bound

Northern Flying Squirrel

Glaucomys sabrinus

A small squirrel, weighing 4 oz (112 g). Its silky fur is olive brown on the back and lead gray on the underside. A fold of skin stretches between front and hind legs and body, forming a "wing" and allowing the squirrel to glide. Its bushy tail is flattened to aid in sailing.

Track: Front foot size of a quarter, with four toes in 1-2-1 grouping. Five toes on hind foot, 1-3-1 grouping. Toes relatively slender. Claws relatively short and may not show. Hind foot interdigital pads form a tight crescent, though proximal pads are lacking.

Trail: Bounding stride averages 20 in (50 cm). Uses a full bound.

Scat: Small, usually unconnected ovals.

Habitat: Deciduous and coniferous forests, though often found in attics of houses.

scat
0.1 in
0.3 cm

Similar species: Differs from all other squirrels and chipmunks by the tight crescent of interdigital pads on the hind foot. Lacks the long claws of prairie dogs and ground squirrels. Smaller than marmot.

Other sign: Skin flap outlines may show in dust or snow. Sometimes builds roof on bird nest to use as den. Tree dens may hold 20 individuals during the winter.

hind prints
on front

**wing
marks**

front
0.5 x 0.5 in
1.3 x 1.3 cm

bound

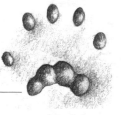

interdigital pads
arrayed in a
crescent shape

hind
1.5 x 0.5 in
3.8 x 1.3 cm

wing
drag

FRONT TRACK LENGTH

FRONT TRACK WIDTH

Northern Pocket Gopher

Thomomys talpoides

Hamster-sized, about 4 oz (112 g), with minute eyes and ears and a short tail. Has external, fur-lined cheek pouches. Color grayish, slightly lighter on belly.

Track: Five toes on front and hind feet. Toes relatively slender. Front foot is relatively long, and has long, wide claws for digging. Claw length is equal to or greater than toe length.

Trail: Walking stride 4 in (10 cm).

Scat: Thick, short cords, about 0.25 in (0.6 cm) long.

Habitat: Meadows, from plains to mountaintops.

Similar species: Differs from other rodents by large, strong claws.

Other sign: Summer soil mounds consist of loose dirt forming a flat mound with no entrance visible (gophers close the tunnel as they go back underground). After snow melt, solid casts of

scat
0.2 in
0.5 cm

SCAT WIDTH

soil and rocks show where gophers packed
dirt into tunnels in the snow while burrowing in the search for food. Scat is often found
embedded in the tunnel casts.

**dirt cast of
winter snow
tunnels**

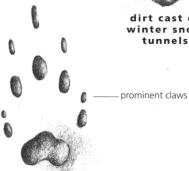

—— prominent claws

fast walk

front
0.6 x 0.5 in
1.5 x 1.3 cm

heel not included in
track measurement

hind
0.75 x 0.5 in
1.9 x 1.3 cm

walk

FRONT TRACK LENGTH

FRONT TRACK WIDTH

Ord's Kangaroo Rat

Dipodomys ordii

Stocky and mouse-sized, about 2 oz (56 g), with large hind feet and long, fur-tipped tail. Reddish brown on back, white side stripe, and dark belly.

Track: Feet have four toes. Long heel on hind foot may register. Feet are furred and toes difficult to distinguish.

Trail: Bounding stride averages 7 in (18 cm) and typically ranges from 8–16 in (20–40 cm). Often bounds on hind feet only. Tail drag often observed.

Scat: Small, usually unconnected ovals.

Habitat: Low-elevation animal. Prefers sandy soil where it can easily dig burrows.

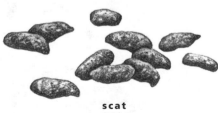

scat
0.2 in
0.5 cm

SCAT WIDTH

Similar species: Track differs from western jumping mouse by greater width and more hair. Bounds on the hind feet only; no front prints visible in the bounding pattern.

Other sign: Scrapes out shallow "bathtubs" in dust as it dusts itself for protection against fleas.

bound on hind feet

tail drag close-up

front
1 x 1.1 in
2.5 x 2.8 cm

long heel, not included in track measurement

hind
1.5 x 0.5 in
3.8 x 1.3 cm

bound

FRONT TRACK LENGTH

FRONT TRACK WIDTH

Beaver
Castor canadensis

Largest rodent in North America, 30–60 lb (14–27 kg). Distinguished by large, webbed hind feet and large, horizontally flattened tail. Fur overall is dark brown to almost black, with lighter belly.

Track: Front and hind prints show five toes. Hind foot may be larger than a human hand. Webbing between hind toes shows, but only when pulled tight by splaying of toes. Clear tracks are difficult to find, as the hind foot steps on the front foot and the dragging tail obliterates many prints.

Trail: Walking stride 18 in (45 cm).

Scat: Seldom found, as they are usually deposited in water, where they disintegrate quickly. Marshmallow-sized, a little longer than thick. Consist of wood chips.

scat
1 x 0.7 in
2.5 x 1.8 cm

wood chips

Habitat: Seldom found far from a creek, river, pond, or lake.

Similar species: Differs from other rodents by large size and webbing. Differs from river otter by long, slender toes and pointed heel, and by lacking a chevron-shaped pad.

Other sign: Dams and conical lodges, built of twigs and sticks. Standing, cut-off tree trunks end in a tapered cone. Debarked tree limbs in the water.

lodge

front
3 x 2.75 in
7.5 x 6.9 cm

web

hind
5 x 5.5 in
12.5 x 13.8 cm

walk

FRONT TRACK LENGTH

FRONT TRACK WIDTH

Field Mouse

Peromyscus species

Deer mouse
P. maniculatus

Small mouse, weighing 0.5 oz (14 g). Adults are reddish brown on back with a white belly, while juveniles are dark gray on the back with a light gray belly. Large eyes and ears. Tail is long and haired.

Track: Track smaller than a dime. Four toes on front foot, in 1-2-1 grouping. Five toes on hind foot, 1-3-1 grouping. Four joined interdigital and two proximal pads on front footprint, five joined pads and heel on hind footprint. Heel is hairless.

Trail: Bounding stride averages 8 in (20 cm). Those species which use a full bound are climbers and nest in grass, shrubs, or trees. Those species using a half bound nest on or below ground. Both types occasionally trot. Tail drag may be present.

Scat: Oval-shaped pellets similar to those left by house mice.

scat
0.1 in
0.3 cm

Habitat: Ubiquitous, being found from deserts to the northern tree line, from below sea level to the top of high peaks.

Similar species: Differs from shrew by having only four toes on the front feet and by being slightly larger. Differs from vole by often showing a tail drag and by most often bounding. Lacks the long heel of the jumping mouse. Smaller than chipmunk.

tail drag

Other sign: Compact grass nests without entrances may be found under logs, rocks, and boards. Enters and exits through the grass wall, which closes up after passage. Caches large quantities of seeds in any convenient protected area. Leaves feces near and in nest.

front
0.3 x 0.3 in
0.8 x 0.8 cm

remnant pad

hind
0.4 x 0.3 in
1 x 0.8 cm

4 x 4 bound

3 x 3 bound

FRONT TRACK LENGTH

FRONT TRACK WIDTH

Bushy-tailed Woodrat
Neotoma cinerea

Rat-sized, with a bushy, squirrel-like tail. Averages about 1 lb (0.5 kg). Dusty brown on back, with gray face and whitish belly. Large eyes and ears. Also known as the pack rat of Western fables.

Track: Four toes on front foot, in 1-2-1 grouping. Five toes on hind foot, 1-3-1 grouping. Toes relatively slender. Toe pads are slightly constricted. Three joined interdigital, one remnant, and two proximal pads on front footprint and four joined pads and two proximal pads on hind. Feet have considerable hair, sometimes making prints appear large and distinct.

Trail: Bounding stride 10 in (25 cm). Walking stride 6 in (15 cm). Bound is probably the most common gait, but walk is also common.

Scat: Small oval pellets.

Habitat: Prefers rocky areas, but will use houses and other human structures when available.

scat
0.2 in
0.5 cm

SCAT WIDTH

Similar species: Larger than mouse and vole. Differs from squirrels by the presence of heel pads on hind foot and by having constricted toe pads.

Other sign: Piles of sticks, cactus, bones, porcupine quills, and other debris tightly wedged in cracks in the rocks identify the pack rat home. Yes, this is where to look for missing keys, rings, glasses, and false teeth.

constricted toe pad

front
0.6 x 0.5 in
1.5 x 1.3 cm

remnant pad

bound

heel not included in track measurement

hind
1.5 x 0.9 in
3.8 x 2.3 cm

fast walk

FRONT TRACK LENGTH

FRONT TRACK WIDTH

Voles
Microtus species

Many species of
mouse-sized mammals,
related to lemmings
and weighing up to
1 oz (28 g). *Microtus*
species are gray to
gray-brown on back,

Mountain vole
M. montanus

with a light colored belly. Small, stocky mammals with short
ears and small eyes, almost hidden by their fur. Short tails are
sparsely haired.

Track: Track smaller than a dime. Four toes
on front foot, in 1-2-1 grouping. Five toes
on hind foot, 1-3-1 grouping. Four joined
interdigital and two proximal pads on front
footprint and four interdigital pads and one
proximal on hind footprint. Heel is hairless.

Trail: Trotting stride 6 in (15 cm). Usually
trot, seldom bound. Tails usually do not show
in the trail.

Scat: Oval-shaped pellets similar to those left by house mice,
often piled in tennis ball–sized latrines which may hold hundreds
of pellets.

scat
0.1 in
0.3 cm

latrine

Habitat: *Microtus* species are grass-loving species, found near meadows across North America and north to the Arctic.

Similar species: Differ from shrews by having only four toes on the front feet. Differ from mice by seldom showing a tail drag and by most often trotting. Lack the long heel of the jumping mouse.

Other sign: As snow melts in the spring, grass nests lacking entrances may be found. Snow melt may also reveal 1 in (2.5 cm) cords of grass and debris, stuffed into snow tunnels during the winter to make space elsewhere in the tunnel network. Vole "latrines" are usually found near nests, while mice leave feces near and in their nests. Worn runways through the grass.

bound

fast trot

trot

front
0.3 x 0.3 in
0.8 x 0.8 cm

hind
0.4 x 0.3 in
1 x 0.8 cm

five pads

heel not included in track measurement

FRONT TRACK LENGTH

FRONT TRACK WIDTH

Muskrat
Ondatra zibethica

Large, rat-like, stocky, up to 4 lb (2 kg). Males are slightly larger than females. Small eyes and ears. Tail is black, flattened, scaly, with few hairs.

Track: Four toes on front foot (small fifth nubbin may show in very clear tracks) and five on hind foot. Toes very slender. Hind foot appears wider than long.

Trail: Walking strides averages 11 in (28 cm). May lope with body turned to side.

Scat: Oval, at most three to four times longer than wide. Often deposited in a sticky mass on exposed logs at water's edge.

scat
0.2 in
0.5 cm

Habitat: Marshes and lake edges, secondarily on stream banks. Large rivers are not as frequently used.

Similar species: Differs from beaver by smaller size and lack of webbing. Differs from mink by long slender toes and by usually walking.

Other sign: Small conical domes made from reeds serve as dens. Cut grass and reeds near water's edge mark feeding sites. Muskrats make "post offices," repeated scat deposits, on rocks.

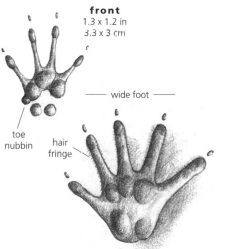

post office

front
1.3 x 1.2 in
3.3 x 3 cm

toe nubbin

hair fringe

—— wide foot ——

hind
1.3 x 1.6 in
3.3 x 4 cm

4 x 4 bound

3 x 3 bound

side lope

fast walk

walk

FRONT TRACK LENGTH

FRONT TRACK WIDTH

Western Jumping Mouse

Zapus princeps

A small—about 1 oz (28 g)—
mouse with long hind feet and
long, sparsely haired tail.
Yellowish sides, darker
yellow-brown back, and
white belly.

Track: Four toes on front foot, in 1-2-1 grouping. Hind foot is about the size of a quarter,
exceptionally long and narrow, and has five
toes in 1-3-1 grouping. Toes relatively slender. Heel is hairless.

Trail: Bounding stride 60–120 in (150–300
cm). Makes sharp turns during travel. May
cover considerable distance per stride when
pursued. Tail drag often observed.

scat
0.1 in
0.3 cm

SCAT WIDTH

Scat: Small oval pellets.

Habitat: Mountains, seldom found more than 3 ft (1 m) from a stream.

Similar species: Differs from other rodents in having long, narrow hind feet and tail drag. Differs from kangaroo rat by bounding from all four feet, not just hind, and in having five toes on hind foot.

Other sign: Small piles of grass stems left after eating. Round grass nests.

tail drag

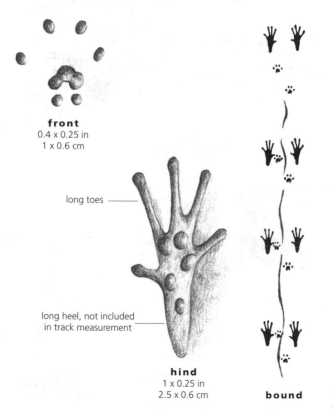

front
0.4 x 0.25 in
1 x 0.6 cm

long toes

long heel, not included in track measurement

hind
1 x 0.25 in
2.5 x 0.6 cm

bound

FRONT TRACK LENGTH

FRONT TRACK WIDTH

Porcupine
Erethizon dorsatum

Basketball-sized
or larger, 10–25 lb
(5–11 kg). Stocky
body, with short
legs. Distinguished
by the presence of
quills. Brown to
yellowish brown in
color.

Track: Rough texture formed by small nubs on soles of feet. Four toes on front foot and five toes on hind. Toes often do not show.

Trail: Walking stride 17 in (43 cm). Tail drag often present.

Scat: Winter scat formed from feeding on conifers is red. Summer scat includes more herbs and shrubs, and is brown to black. Scat

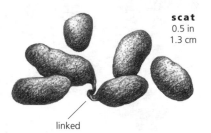

scat
0.5 in
1.3 cm

linked

**debarked
stick with
chew marks**

from both seasons may be composed of individual pellets or strings of pellets connected by fibers.

Habitat: Generally found near forests, but may be far from trees if shrubs are available.

Similar species: Rough texture on sole of foot is diagnostic. In snow, trough made by dragging belly highlights its stockiness, separating it from faster-moving mammals.

Other sign: Twigs with bark chewed off, found at the bases of trees. Will perch in a tree for days, chewing the bark, thereby killing the tree.

tail drag

fast walk

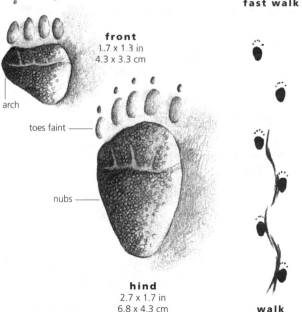

front
1.7 x 1.3 in
4.3 x 3.3 cm

arch

toes faint —

nubs —

hind
2.7 x 1.7 in
6.8 x 4.3 cm

walk

FRONT TRACK LENGTH

FRONT TRACK WIDTH

White-tailed Deer

Odocoileus virginianus

Smallest member of the
deer family. Male averages
130 lb (60 kg), female
about 110 lb (50 kg). Coat
is reddish in summer and
blue-gray in winter. The
prominent white tail is
carried erect when animal
disturbed. Antlers, found
only on male, have *tines*, or
points, branching off main
beam.

Track: Heart-shaped, with convex wall. Pad
occupies most of the clout; subunguinis slender.

Trail: Walking stride 30 in (75 cm). Pronks
or stots with front and hind feet striking the
ground at the same time. Gallops when in
a hurry.

Scat: Usually dry, falls apart when it hits the
ground. Pellets vary from nipple-dimple shape to oval.

nipple   dimple

scat
pellet 0.3 in
pellet 0.8 cm

antler

SCAT WIDTH

Habitat: Generally closed timber, but moves out to grasslands at twilight to feed.

Similar species: Track is not distinguishable from mule deer, although whitetail is usually smaller in most geographic areas. Differs from pronghorn, goats, and sheep by having convex walls. Smaller than elk, has more slender tips, and pad occupies most of clout.

Other sign: Gathers ("yards up") in large numbers in sheltered groves during the winter. Breaks off limbs of trees when removing the velvet from antlers. Velvet is difficult to find, as both deer and rodents eat the nutrient-rich material. Height of tree wound indicates animal height.

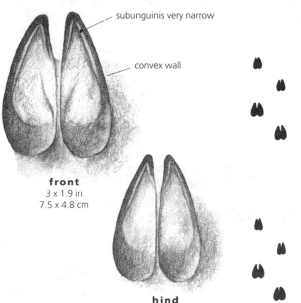

subunguinis very narrow

convex wall

front
3 x 1.9 in
7.5 x 4.8 cm

hind
2.6 x 1.5 in
6.5 x 3.8 cm

pronk

gallop

FRONT TRACK LENGTH

FRONT TRACK WIDTH

Mule Deer
Odocoileus hemionus

Small member of the
deer family, male
averaging 160 lb
(70 kg) and female
about 130 lb (60 kg).
Coat color is reddish
brown in summer and
grayish brown in the
winter. Antlers, found
only on males, branch
symmetrically and are
shed annually.

Track: Heart-shaped, with convex wall. Pad occupies most of the clout; subunguinis slender.

Trail: Walking stride 36 in (90 cm). Pronks or stots with front and hind feet striking the ground at the same time. Gallops when in a hurry.

Scat: Usually dry, falls apart when it hits the ground. Pellets vary from nipple-dimple shape to oval.

scat
pellet 0.3 in
pellet 0.8 cm

nipple

dimple

antler

SCAT WIDTH

Habitat: Foothills are prime habitat, where can frequent open brush interspersed with rugged terrain. Found in all vegetation zones except in the Arctic and in extreme desert.

Similar species: Track is not distinguishable from white-tailed deer, although mule deer is usually larger in most geographic areas. Differs from pronghorn, goats, and sheep by having convex walls. Smaller than elk, has more slender tips, and pad occupies most of clout.

Other sign: Breaks off limbs of trees when removing the velvet from antlers. Velvet is difficult to find, as both deer and rodents eat the nutrient-rich material. Height of tree wound indicates height of animal.

pronk

subunguinis very narrow

convex wall

front
3.25 x 2.6 in
8.1 x 6.5 cm

hind
3.1 x 2.5 in
7.8 x 6.3 cm

gallop

FRONT TRACK LENGTH

FRONT TRACK WIDTH

Elk

Cervus elaphus

Medium-sized, larger than deer, males averaging 700 lb (315 kg) and females 450 lb (200 kg). Reddish to dark brown, with a yellow rump patch. Males have antlers that are shed annually. Also known as wapiti.

Track: Blocky, with each clout wide at the leading tip. Pad of hoof occupies rear third of each clout; subunguinis occupies remaining two-thirds of each clout.

Trail: Walking stride 52 in (130 cm). When chased by a predator, gallops and—occasionally—pronks.

Scat: Most of the year, scat consists of pellets that scatter on impact with the ground. When the diet is moist, nipple-dimple shape predominates, changing to oval as

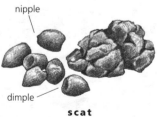

nipple

dimple

scat
pellet 0.5 in
pellet 1.3 cm

antler

drying of vegetation occurs. When scat is moist, pellets stick together.

Habitat: Forest. Beds in dense trees during the day, moving out into clearings to graze during twilight hours.

pronk

Similar species: Differs from deer and moose by having a small pad at the rear of the hoof. Differs from bighorn sheep and antelope by having walls that bend to the outside of each clout.

Other sign: In removing velvet from their antlers, bulls strip bark from young saplings and break off limbs, often killing the trees. Height of tree wound shows animal height. Bulls make mud wallows in the fall. During rut, look for areas where bulls have sparred with the ground using their antlers.

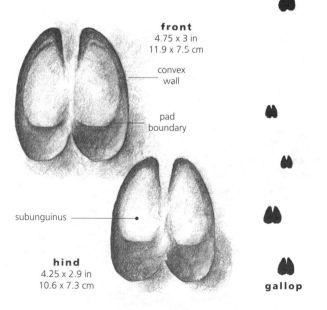

front
4.75 x 3 in
11.9 x 7.5 cm

convex wall

pad boundary

subunguinus

hind
4.25 x 2.9 in
10.6 x 7.3 cm

gallop

FRONT TRACK LENGTH

FRONT TRACK WIDTH

Pronghorn Antelope
Antilocapra americana

Smaller than deer, found only in North America. Male averages 125 lb (56 kg), female about 110 lb (50 kg). White and tan to reddish brown, with black and brown markings on the head and neck. Both sexes have forked horns that are shed annually.

Track: Identified by the concave outline of the wall, which bends slightly inward at a point about one-third of the way back from the tip. Pad is bulbous. Lacks dewclaws.

Trail: Ambling stride 35 in (88 cm). Most common gait is an *amble*, a fast walk where the hind foot registers slightly in front of the front footprint. Often uses a Z-shaped gallop, with a stride ranging from 80–145 in (200–363 cm).

scat
pellet 0.3 in
pellet 0.8 cm

SCAT WIDTH

paw mark

urine

scat

"spud"

Scat: Typically, well-defined pellets that often stay together upon impact with the ground.

Habitat: Open and shrub country of short- to mid-grass prairie. Herbs and winter browse above the snow are important. Commonly found with sagebrush.

Similar species: Differentiated from deer by its small size and concave wall. Lacks dewclaws.

Other sign: The territorial marking of the male pronghorn is a *spud*, produced as the male sniffs and paws the ground after urinating and defecating to spread the odor.

gallop

front
2.75 x 2.25 in
6.9 x 5.6 cm

concave wall

bulbous pad

hind
2.25 x 2 in
5.6 x 5 cm

amble

FRONT TRACK LENGTH

FRONT TRACK WIDTH

Bighorn Sheep

Ovis canadensis

Bighorn sheep
O. canadensis

Medium-sized sheep, distinguished by massive horns of the male. Male averages 300 lb (135 kg), female about 200 lb (90 kg). Light brown, white rump and muzzle. Ram has spiraled horn; ewe's is small and straight. Horns are not forked and are never shed. Thinhorn sheep, *O. dalli*, have horns of smaller diameter; body color may be white (Dall sheep) or dark brown (stone sheep).

Track: Blocky, with edges of the walls straight along the sides.

Trail: Trotting stride 70 in (175 cm). Most common gait is a walk with 36 in (90 cm) stride, but trotting is common in open country.

Scat: More likely to be dry and to separate into pellets than that of other hoofed mammals.

Habitat: High mountain areas, especially along cliffs. Comes down from cliffs for water, and grazes on grass in rolling hills. Migrates below timberline during the winter.

(map labels: O. dalli, O. canadensis)

scat
pellet 0.3 in
pellet 0.8 cm

Similar species: Wall differs from antelope and deer by having a straight edge. Shows dewclaws, which antelope does not. Differs from deer and elk by relatively large subunguinis region of the clout.

Other sign: Beds scraped in soil along the edges of cliffs; deposits of old scat at repeatedly used beds may be considerable. Mineral and salt licks often serve as a focus of activity.

**male
horn**

**female
horn**

(O. canadensis)

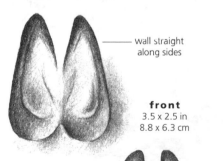

—— wall straight
along sides

front
3.5 x 2.5 in
8.8 x 6.3 cm

hind
3 x 2 in
7.5 x 5 cm

trot

Mountain Goat
Oreamnos americanus

Sheep-sized mammal, found only in North America. Male averages 300 lb (135 kg), female about 200 lb (90 kg). Predominantly white, and distinguished by a stocky build and hump on shoulders. Horns, which are not shed, are straight, about 10 in (25 cm); those of female slightly smaller.

Track: Footprint is blocky. Tip of the clout occurs in the middle of each clout, not to the inside as in other hoofed mammals. Relatively large subunguinus.

Trail: Walking stride about 30 in (75 cm). Goats most often walk.

Scat: Tends to be dry and separate when it hits the ground.

scat
pellet 0.4 in
pellet 1 cm

horn

SCAT WIDTH

Habitat: High mountains, on the steepest crags and cliffs. May bed among rocks, or in snowbanks or vegetated areas. Caves may be used as shelter from sun or wind. Wind-blown slopes are used for feeding in the winter.

Similar species: Differs from all other hoofed mammals by the location of tip in the middle of each clout.

Other sign: Digs dry wallows (shallow depressions) in the summer. Mineral or salt licks attract activity.

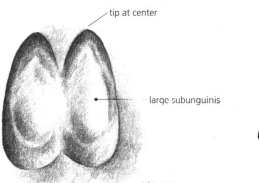

tip at center

large subunguinis

front
3 x 1.9 in
7.5 x 4.8 cm

hind
2.6 x 1.5 in
6.5 x 3.8 cm

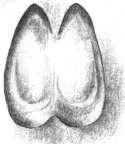

walk

FRONT TRACK LENGTH

FRONT TRACK WIDTH

Selected reading

Tracks and Tracking

Bang, P. et al. 1972. *Collins Guide to Animal Tracks and Signs.* London: Collins Sons.

Brown, R., J. Ferguson, M. Lawrence, and D. Lees. 1987. *Tracks and Signs of the Birds of Britain and Europe: An Identification Guide.* Kent, England: Christopher Helm.

Brunner, J. 1909. *Tracks and Tracking.* New York: Outing.

Fjelline, D. P. and T. M. Mansfield. 1989. Method to standardize the procedure for measuring mountain lion tracks. In *Proceedings of the Third Mountain Lion Workshop,* ed. R.H. Smith, 49–51. Prescott, Ariz.: Arizona Game and Fish Department.

Forrest, L. R. 1988. *Field Guide to Tracking Animals in Snow.* Harrisburg, Penn.: Stackpole Books.

Halfpenny, J. C. 1997. *Tracking: Mastering the Basics.* 180 min. A Naturalist's World. Videocassette.

———— 1986a. A *Field Guide to Mammal Tracking in North America.* Boulder, Colo.: Johnson.

———— 1986b. *Tracks and Tracking: A "How To" Guide.* Gardiner, Mont.: A Naturalist's World. Slides.

Halfpenny, J. C. et al. 1996. Snow tracking. In *American Marten, Fisher, Lynx, and Wolverines: Survey Methods for Their Detection,* ed. W. Zielinski and T. Kucera, 91–163. General Technical Report PSW-GTR-157. Berkeley, Calif.: USDA Forest Service, Pacific Southwest Research Station.

Headstrom, R. 1971. *Identifying Animals Tracks: Mammals, Birds, and Other Animals of the Eastern United States.* New York: Dover.

Murie, O. 1954. *A Field Guide to Animal Tracks.* Peterson Field Guide Series, no. 9. Boston: Houghton Mifflin.

Rezendes, P. 1992. *Tracking and the Art of Seeing: How to Read Animal Tracks and Sign.* Charlotte, Vt.: Camden House.

Seton, E. T. 1958. *Animal Tracks and Hunter Signs.* New York: Doubleday.

Recommended field identification guides

Burt, W. H. and R. P. Grossenheider. 1964. *A Field Guide to the Mammals.* Peterson Field Guide Series, no. 5. Boston: Houghton Mifflin.

Chandlers, S. R., B. Bruun, H. S. Zim. 1983. *A Guide to Field Identification: Birds of North America.* New York: Golden.

National Geographic Society. 1983. *Field Guide to the Birds of North America.* Washington, D.C.: National Geographic Society.

Stebbins, R. C. 1966. *A Field Guide to Western Reptiles and Amphibians.* Peterson Field Guide Series, no. 16. Boston: Houghton Mifflin.

Index

About the author

JAMES HALFPENNY has searched for dinosaur tracks in Colorado and Montana, tracked wildlife in Tanzania and Kenya, studied endangered species on China's Tibet-Qinghai plateau, and researched the polar bears of Hudson Bay and Greenland. Since 1961 he has taught outdoor and environmental education for a vast array of schools and organizations, including the Smithsonian, National Outdoor Leadership School, Outward Bound, the Appalachian Mountain Club, The Wilderness Society, and National Audubon Society. He has trained rangers in tracking techniques at Yellowstone, Glacier, Grand Teton, and Rocky Mountain national parks. His research has also taken him to Antarctica and all over North America. Halfpenny has been featured, with Australian aborigines, Kalahari Bushmen, and Alaskan Inuits, in a documentary about the loss of native tracking skills shown on the Discovery Channel. He is a past field director and project coordinator for the University of Colorado's Institute of Arctic and Alpine Research. He is author of *A Field Guide to Mammal Tracking in North America, Yellowstone Wolves: Watcher's Guide,* and *Winter: an Ecological Handbook.* He lives just outside Yellowstone National Park in Gardiner, Montana.

TODD TELANDER is a freelance natural science illustrator and wildlife artist. He studied biology and environmental studies at the University of California, Santa Cruz, where he became interested in illustration. His work appears in Falcon's *America's 100 Most Wanted Birds, Birder's Dictionary,* and *A Field Guide to Cows* as well as in museums, galleries, and private collections. Telander lives in Taos, New Mexico.